I0494681

St. Marys Ontario Book 1 in Colour Photos, Saving Our History One Photo at a Time

Photography
by Barbara Raué
2015

Series Name:
Cruising Ontario

Book 129: St. Marys Book 1

Cover photo: 236 Jones Street East, Page 44

Series Name: Cruising Ontario
Saving Our History One Photo at a Time
in colour photos

Books Available in Alphabetical Order:
Aberfoyle, Acton, Alton, Ancaster, Arthur, Aylmer, Ayr, Bloomingdale, Brantford, Burlington, Caledon, Caledonia, Cambridge, Clifford, Conestogo, Delhi, Dorchester to Aylmer, Drayton, Drumbo, Dundas, Eden Mills, Elmira, Elora, Fergus, Guelph, Hagersville, Hamilton, Hanover, Harriston, Hespeler, Jarvis, Kitchener, Linwood, Listowel, London, Lucknow, Mono, Mount Forest, Neustadt, New Hamburg, Niagara-on-the-Lake, Oakville, Orangeville, Orillia, Owen Sound, Palmerston, Peterborough, Port Elgin, Preston, Rockwood, Seaforth, Sheffield, Shelburne, Simcoe, Southampton, St. Jacobs, St. Thomas, Stoney Creek, Stratford, Tillsonburg, Waterdown, Waterford, Waterloo, Wellesley, Wingham

Book 110:Lucknow,Mitchell
Book 111: Conestogo, Bloomingdale
Book 112: Delhi
Book 113: Waterford
Book 114-116: Waterloo
Book 117-119: Windsor
Book 120-121: Amherstburg
Book 122: Essex
Book 123-124: Kingsville
Book 125-127: Woodstock
Book 128: Thamesford
Book 129-132: St. Marys

Other Books by Barbara Raue

Coins of Gold

Arrows, Indians and Love

The Life and Times of Barbara
Volume 1: Inventions That Have Enhanced My Life
Volume 2: Entertainment That I Have Enjoyed
Volume 3: East Coast Trips
Volume 4: Olympics Have Always Intrigued Me
Volume 5: Wonders of the World
Volume 6: Caribbean Cruises We Have Enjoyed
Volume 7: Animals
Volume 8: Storms and Other Major Disasters in My Lifetime
Volume 9: Wars, Terrorist Attacks and Major Disasters

The Cromwell Family Book

Laura Secord Discovered

Daddy Where Are You?

Visit Barbara's website to view all of her books
http://barbararaue.ca

Table of Contents

St. Marys is a town in southwestern Ontario located southwest of Stratford. The north branch of the Thames River flows through St. Marys and is the heart of the town. St. Marys' early economic success depended on the mills, powered by the water in this river. The town's prosperity was also helped by the presence of accessible limestone, taken in blocks from the riverbed and from quarries along the riverbanks. The name "Stonetown" is an apt moniker for St. Marys, as the town is filled with unique architecture featuring locally-quarried limestone. The stone buildings reveal much about the town's history, and the development of the town can be witnessed in the architecture.

John Grieve Lind (1867-1947) was closely associated with the start of the St. Mary's Cement Company. St. Marys was chosen as the location for the plant because of its abundance of limestone, clay and water, it was on two national railway lines, and it had access to hydro-electric power from Niagara Falls. The plant opened in 1912.

Once the cement plant was in operation, Lind turned his attention to parks and recreation. He purchased the seven acre Cadzow Park on Church Street South and build Cadzow Pool. Lind Park now contains a statue of Arthur Meighen, Canada's ninth prime minister.

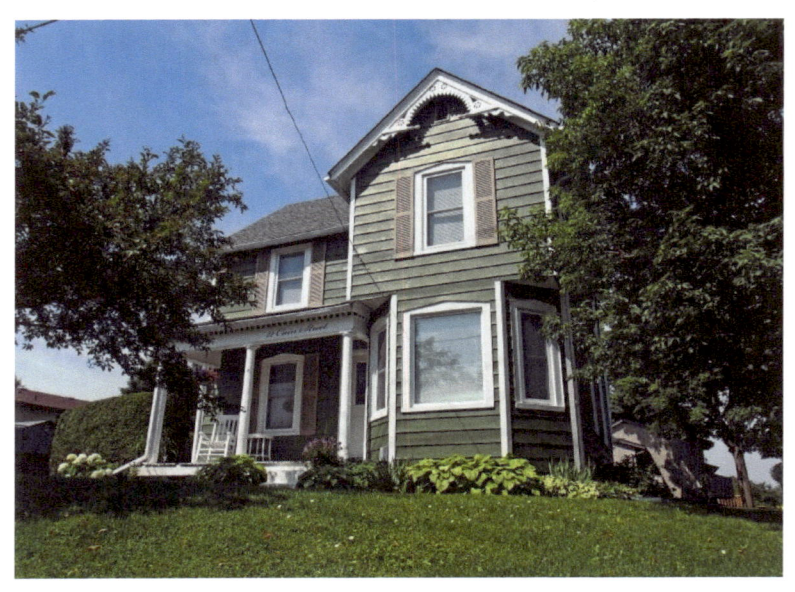

12 Cain Street

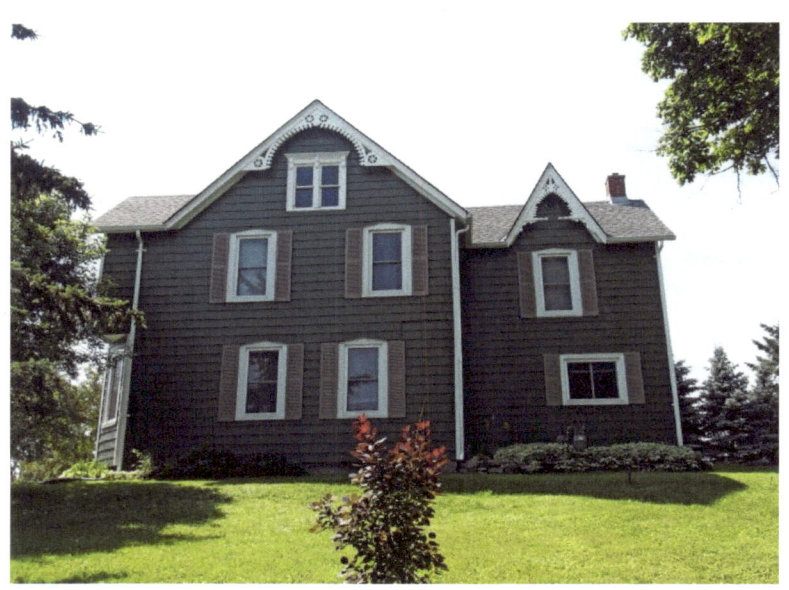

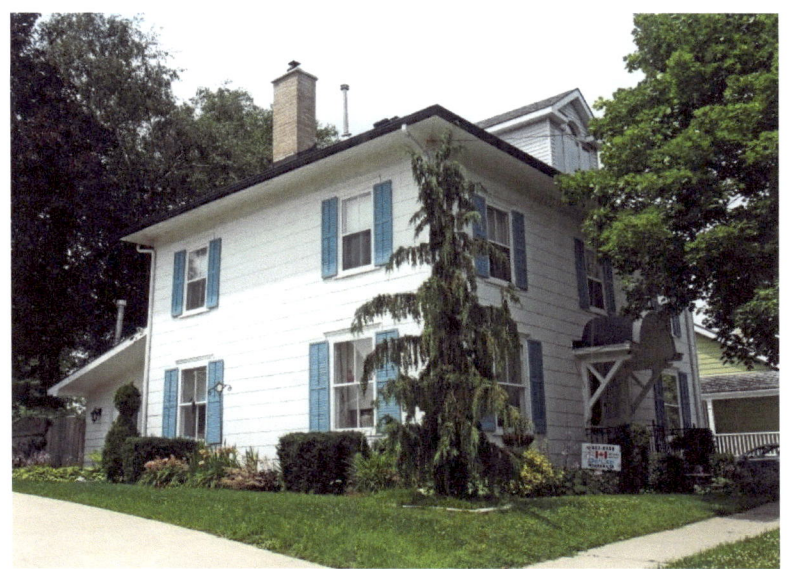

140 Church Street North – Georgian style, dormer on roof

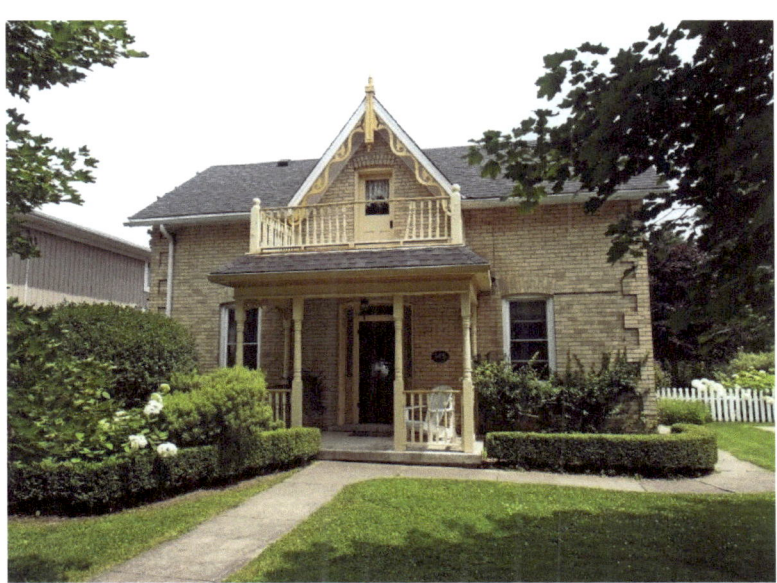

145 Church Street North – Gothic Revival, verge board trim
and finial on gable, corner quoins, wood turned porch
supports, sidelights and transom window surrounding door

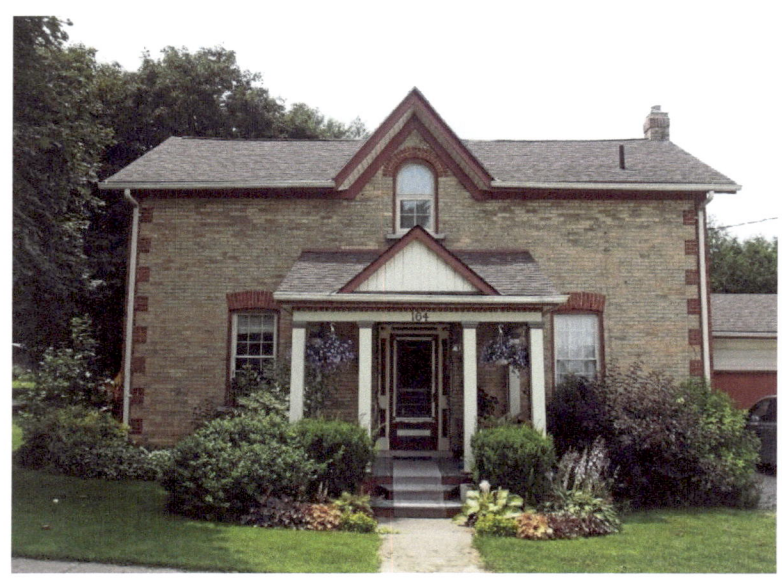

164 Church Street North – Gothic Revival, corner quoins, pediment

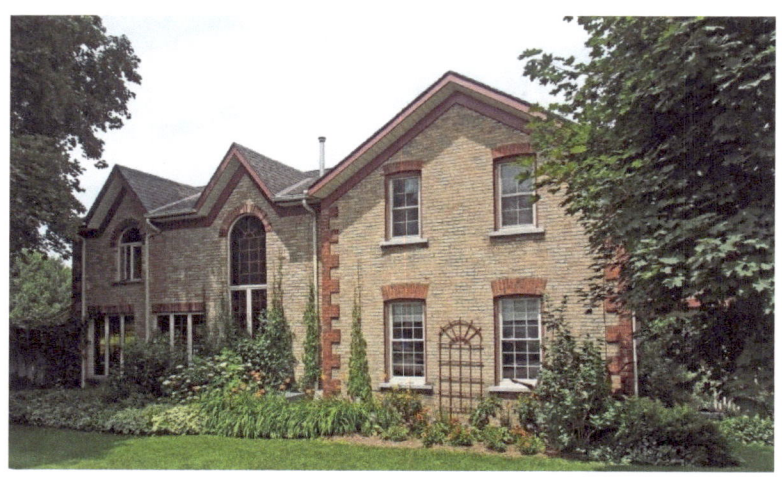

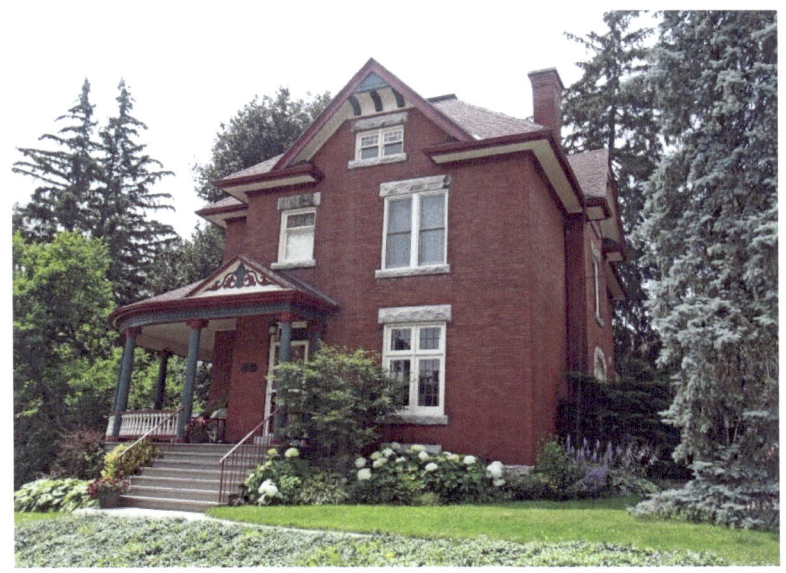

112 Church Street North – pediment with decorated
tympanum

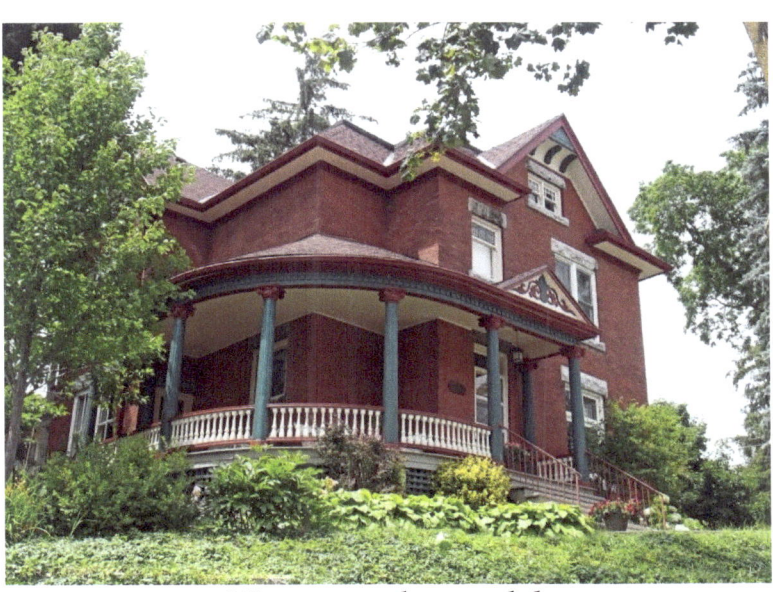

Wraparound verandah

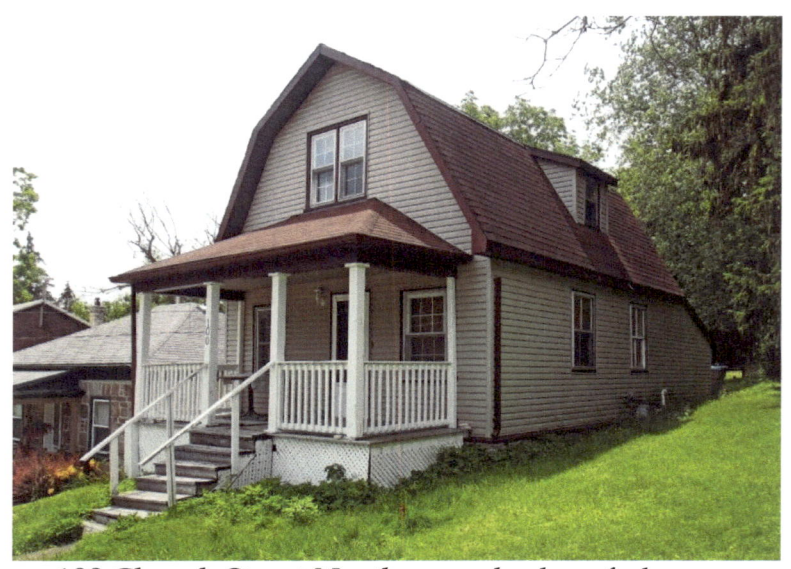

100 Church Street North – gambrel roof, dormer

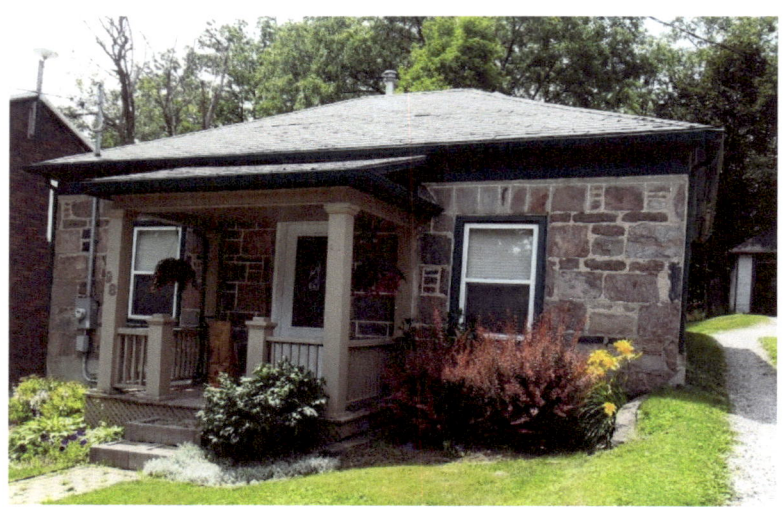

98 Church Street North – Regency cottage – cobblestone
architecture, hipped roof

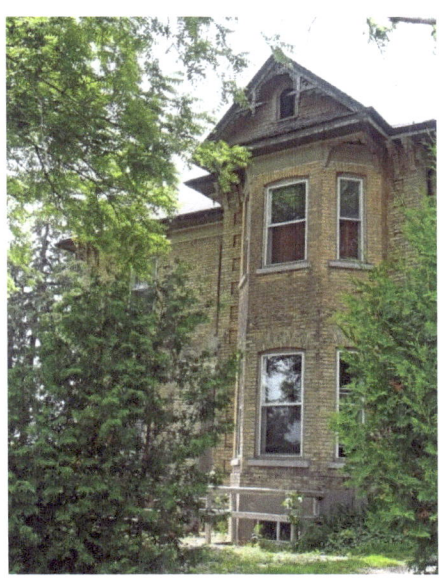

84 Church Street North – Dr. Sparks – Italianate, 2½ storey tower-like bay, corner quoins, cornice brackets, bargeboard on gable, fish scale patterning

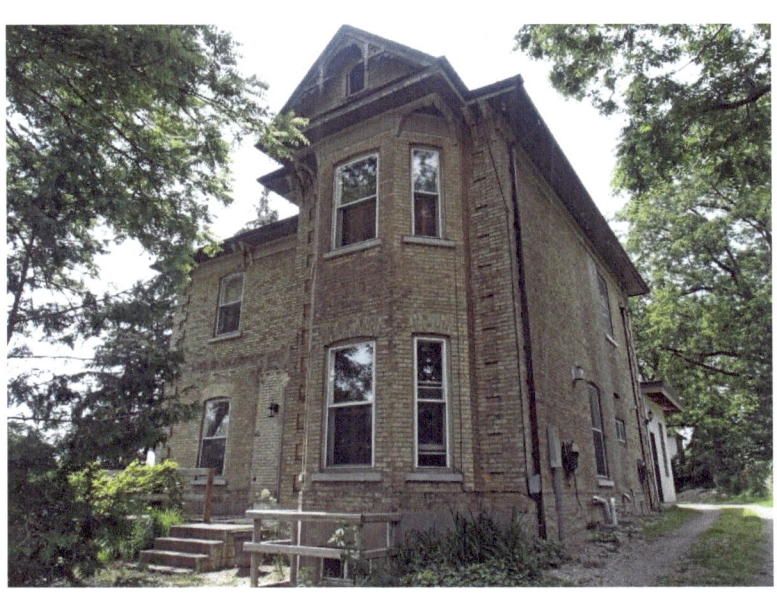

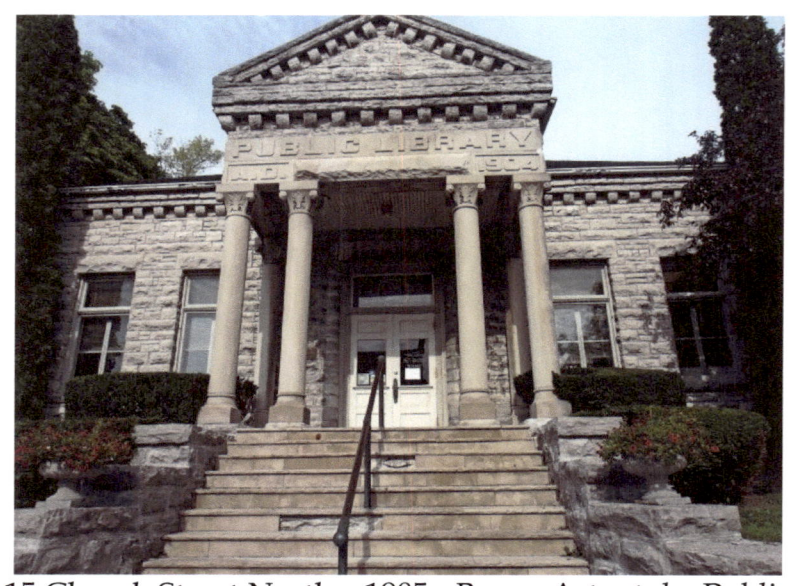

15 Church Street North – 1905 - Beaux Arts style, Public Library built of St. Marys limestone – pediment with dentil moulding, pillars with Corinthian capitals

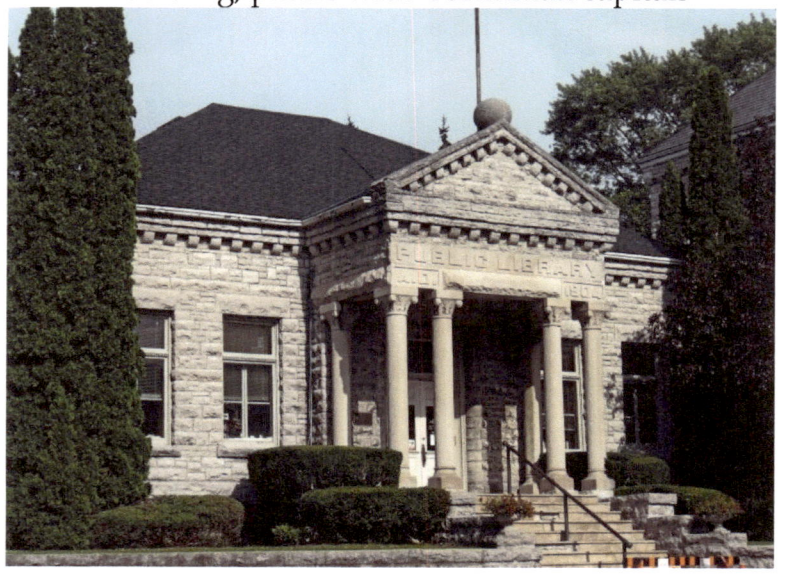

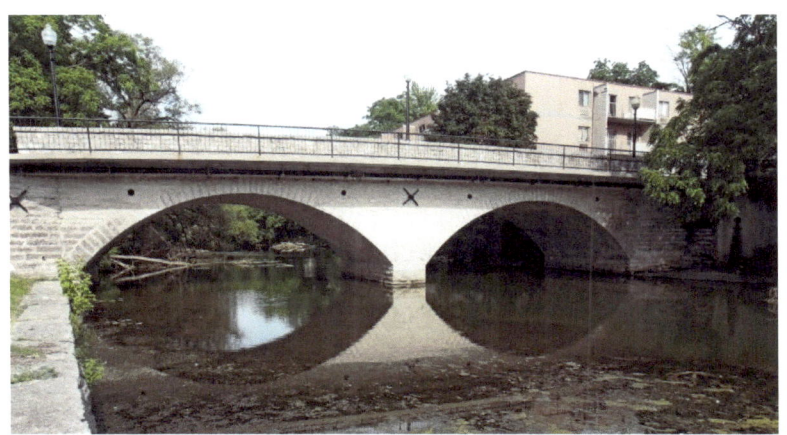

Church Street Bridge – built by local stone masons and completed in 1884 (restored in 1979)

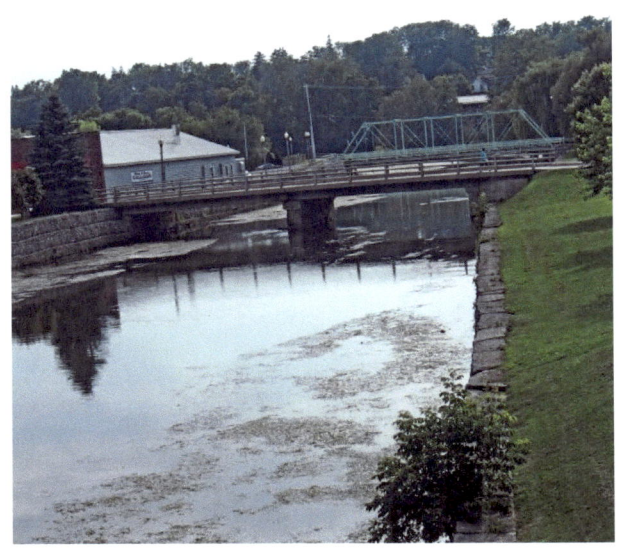

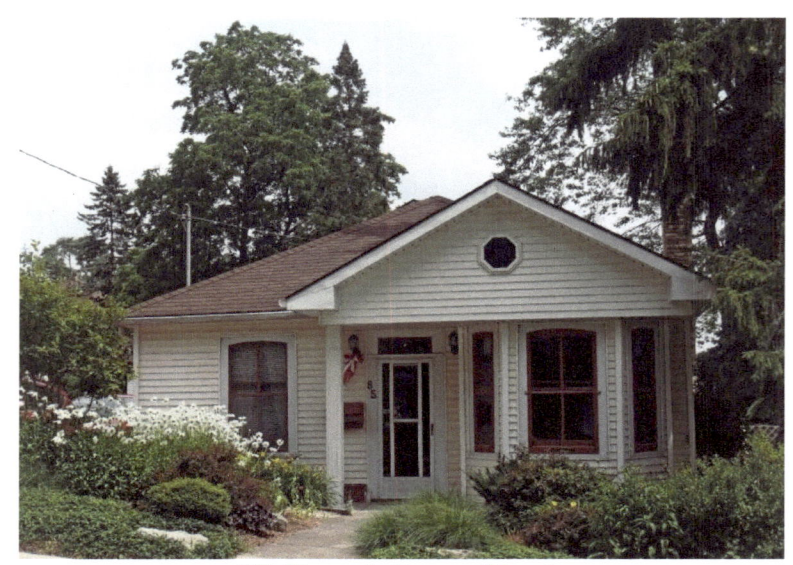

85 Church Street North

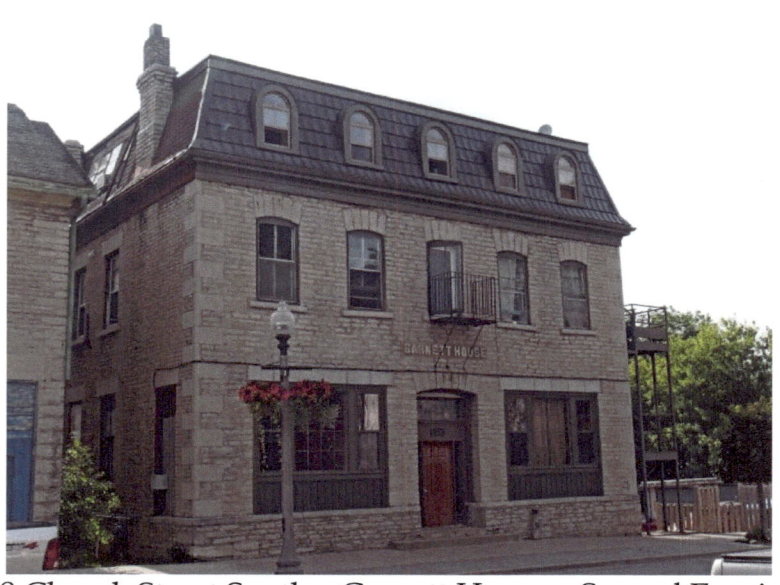

18 Church Street South – Garnett House – Second Empire
style, mansard roof, corner quoins

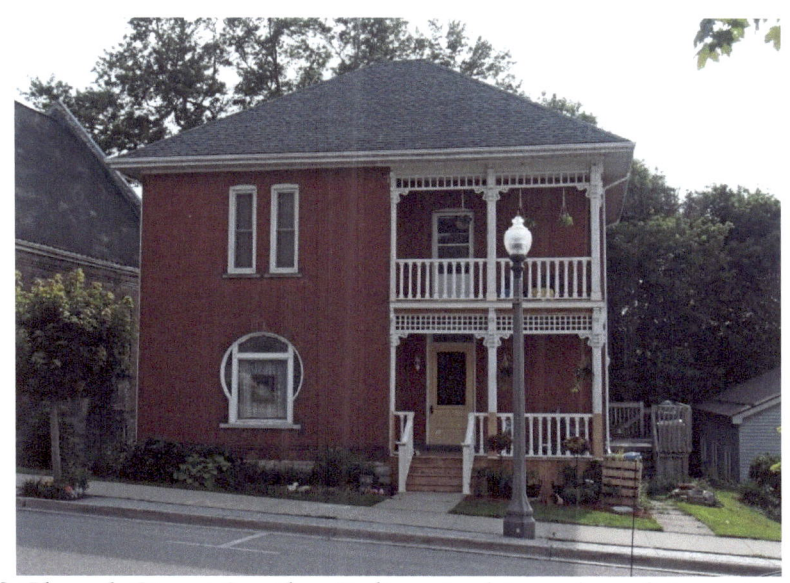

28 Church Street South – Italianate, hipped roof, two-storey porch

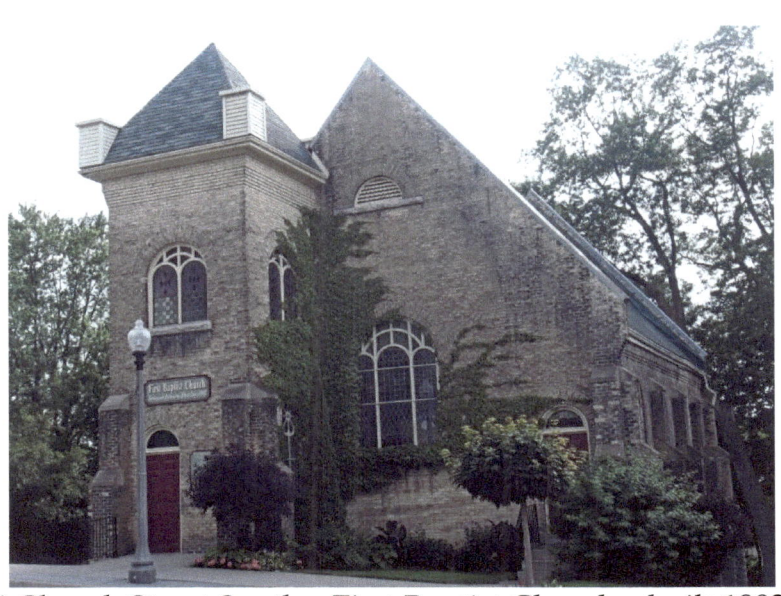

34 Church Street South – First Baptist Church – built 1902 – Romanesque style

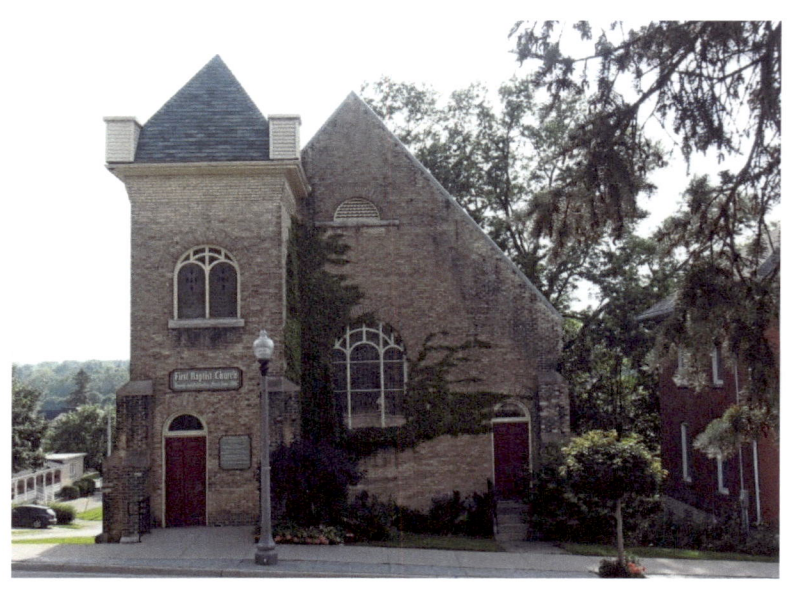

34 Church Street South – First Baptist Church

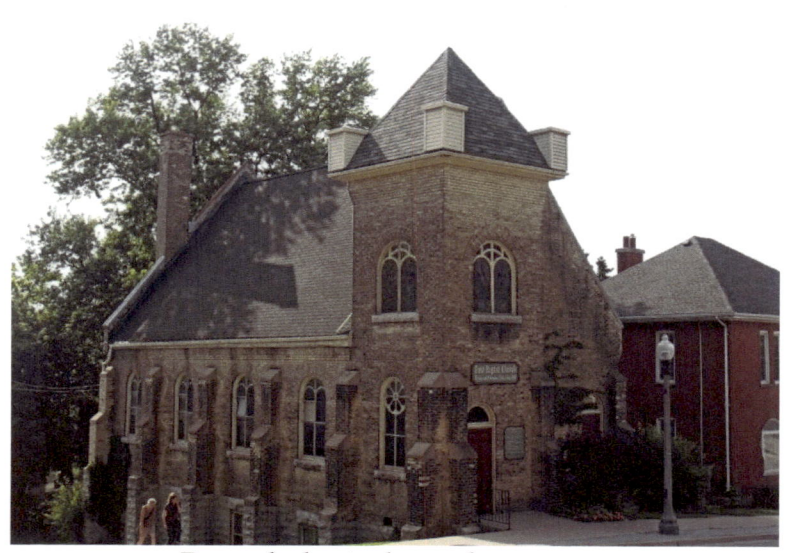

Rounded windows, buttresses

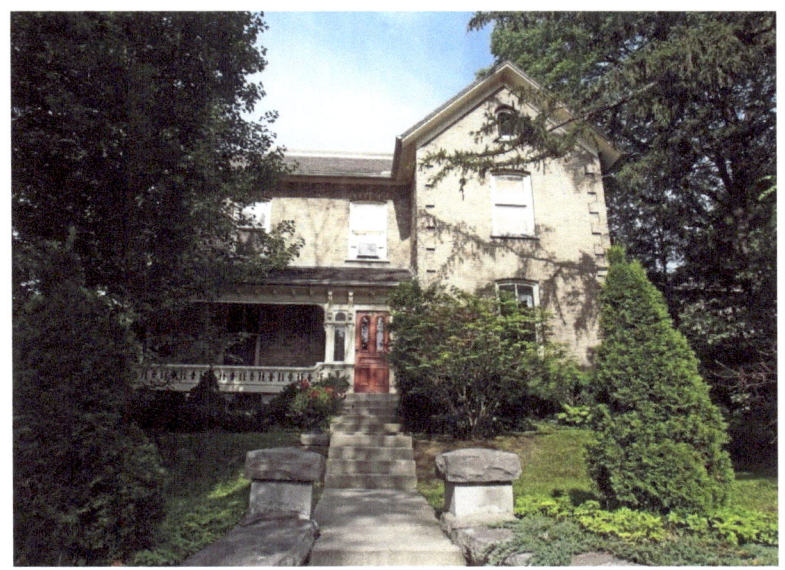

45 Church Street South – Gothic – corner quoins

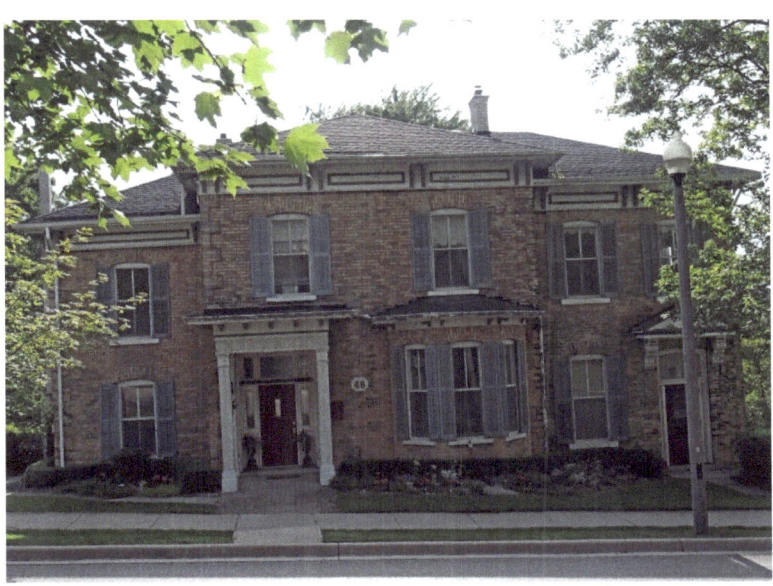

46 Church Street South – Italianate – 1871 - bay window, decorative cornice, entrance, cornice brackets, sidelights and transom around door

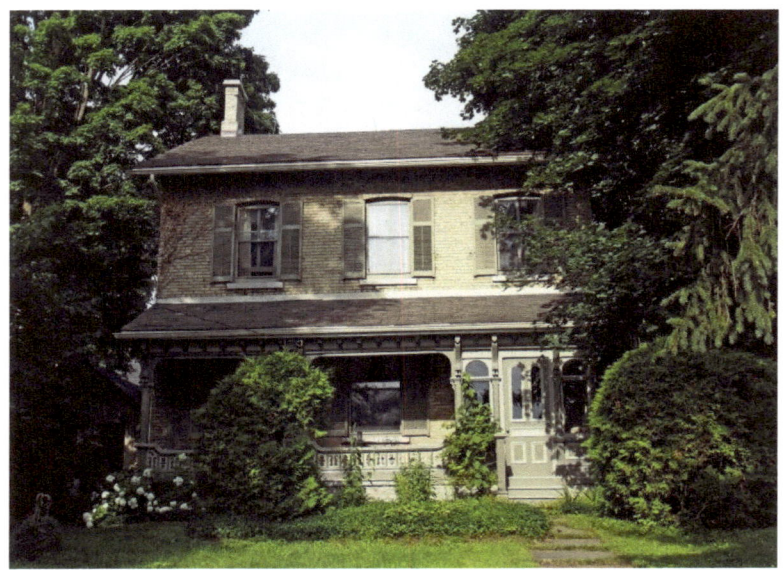

51 Church Street South

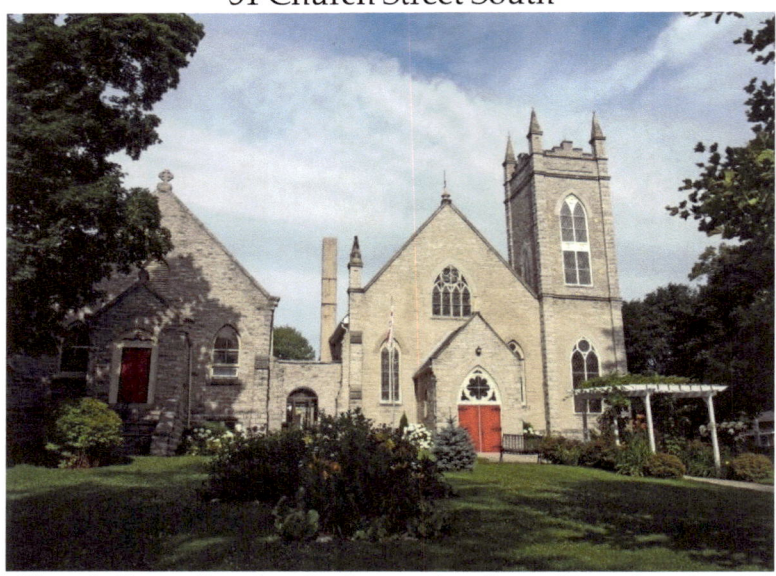

65 Church Street South – St. James Anglican Church – the oldest portion was built in the late 1850s from St. Marys' limestone; in the mid-1880s the roof was raised and the square tower, buttresses and west entrance porch were added; the parish hall was added in 1907

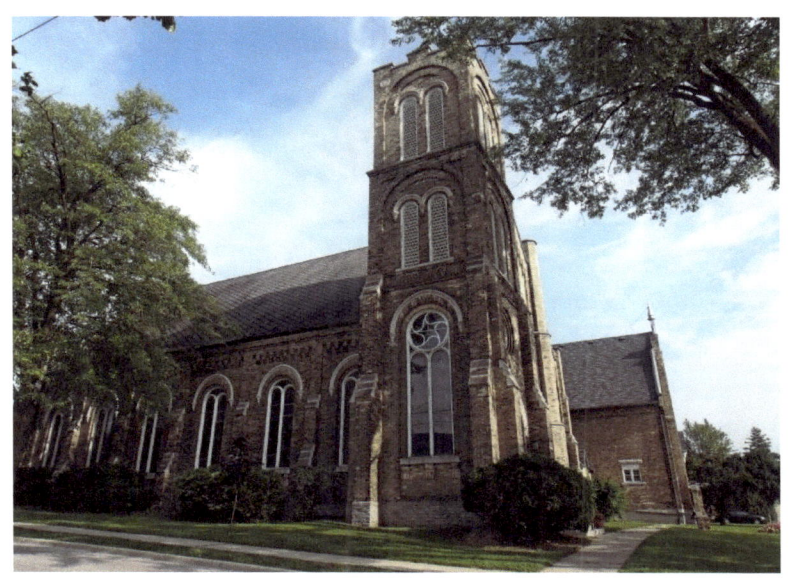

85 Church Street South – St Marys United Church – built in 1879 – yellow Ontario brick – Romanesque style

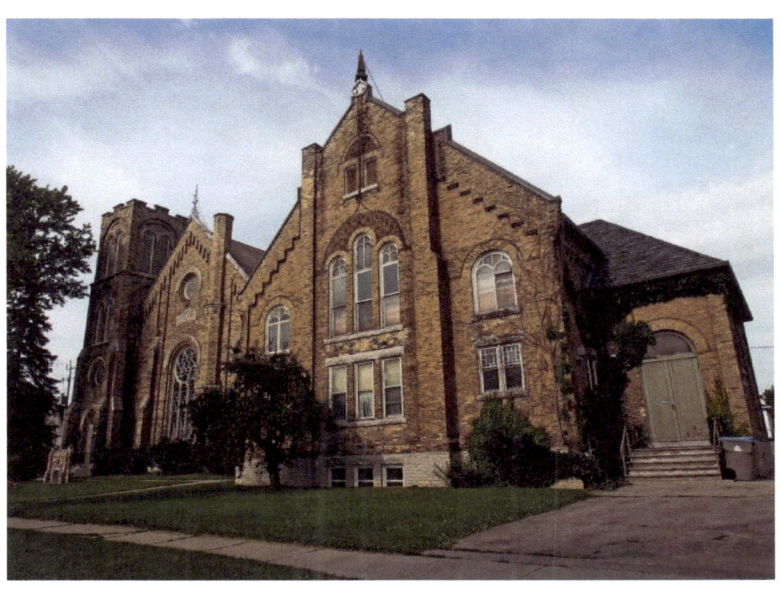

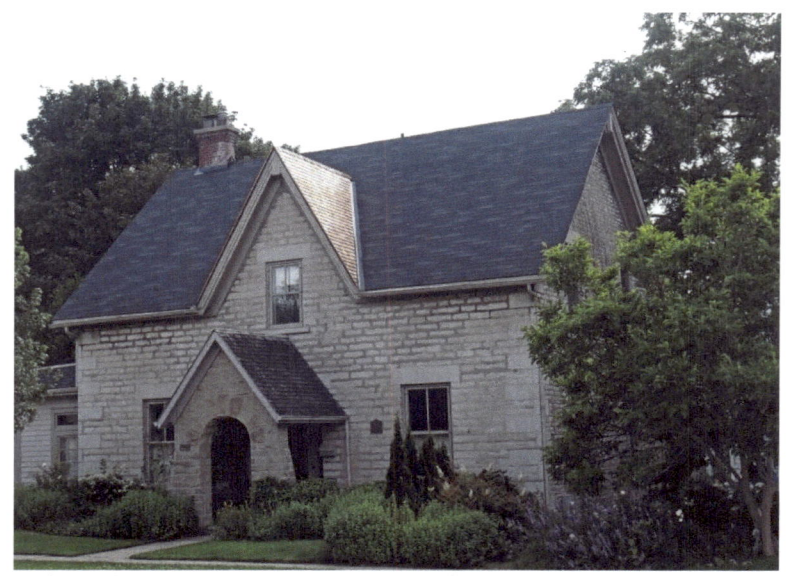

100 Church Street South – home of James Eaton, built in 1863

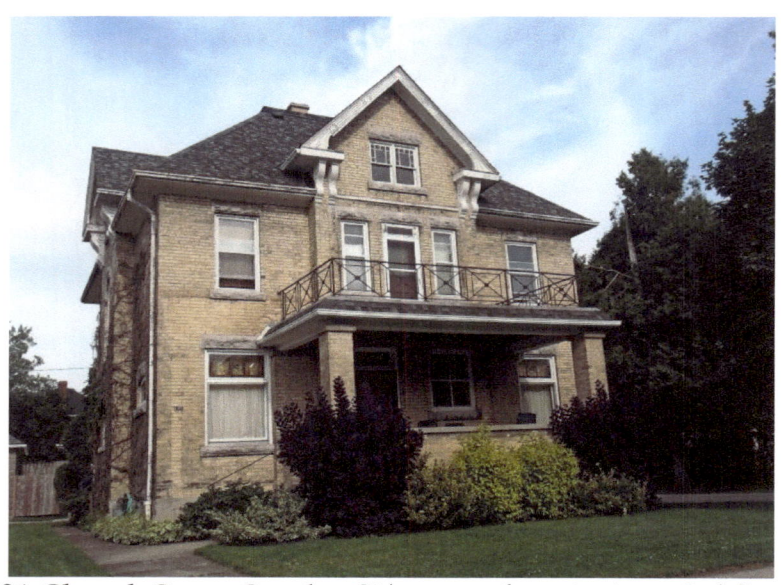

101 Church Street South – 2½ storey frontispiece, 2nd floor balcony

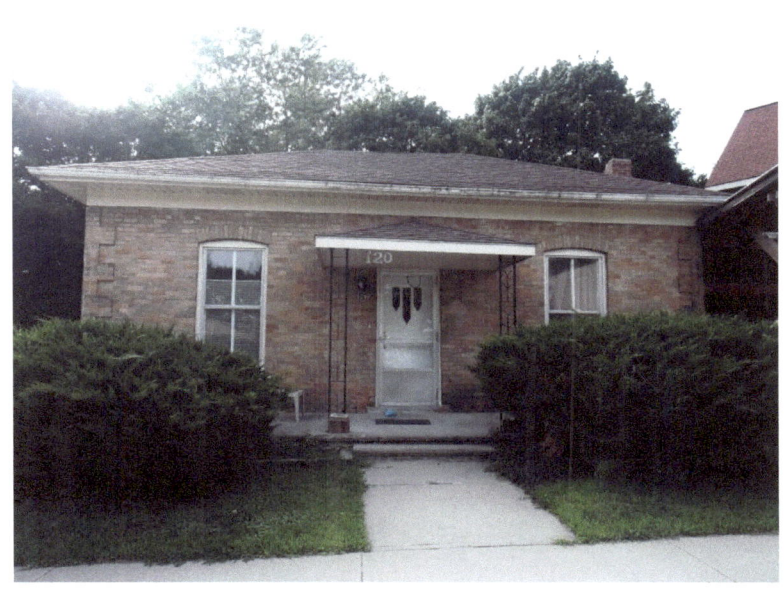

120 Church Street South

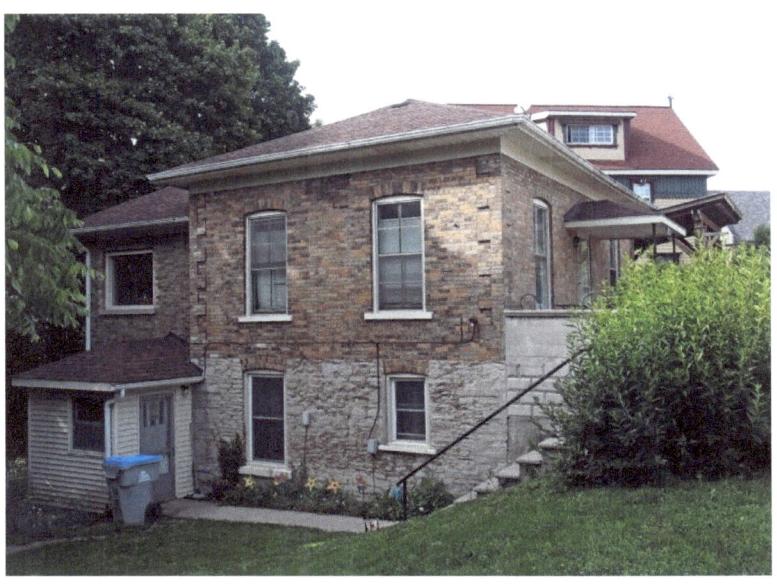

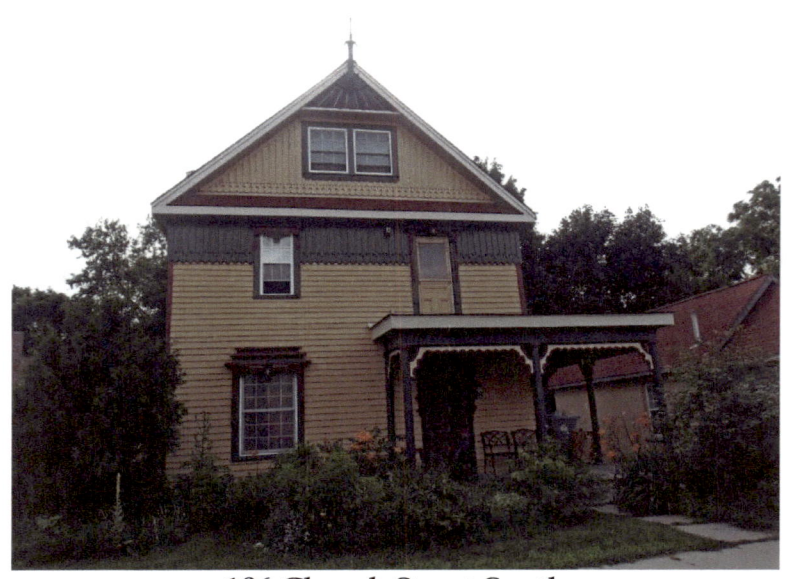

106 Church Street South

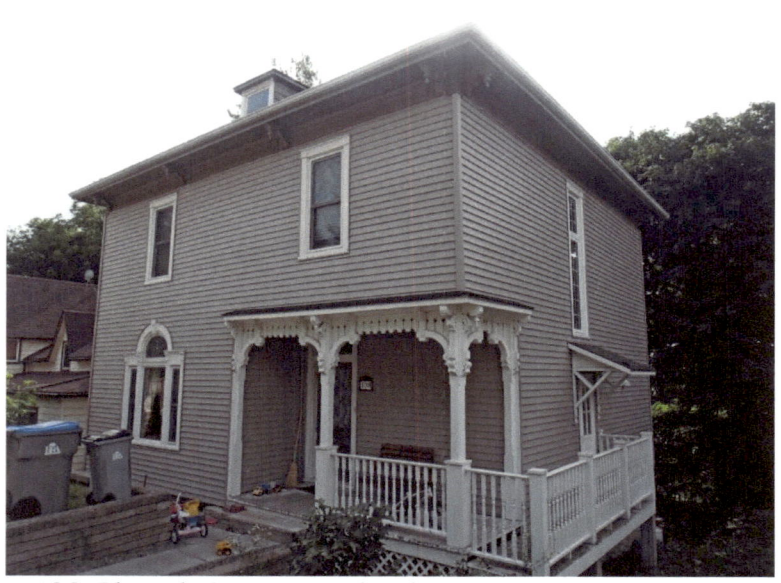

138 Church Street South – bric-a-brac on the porch

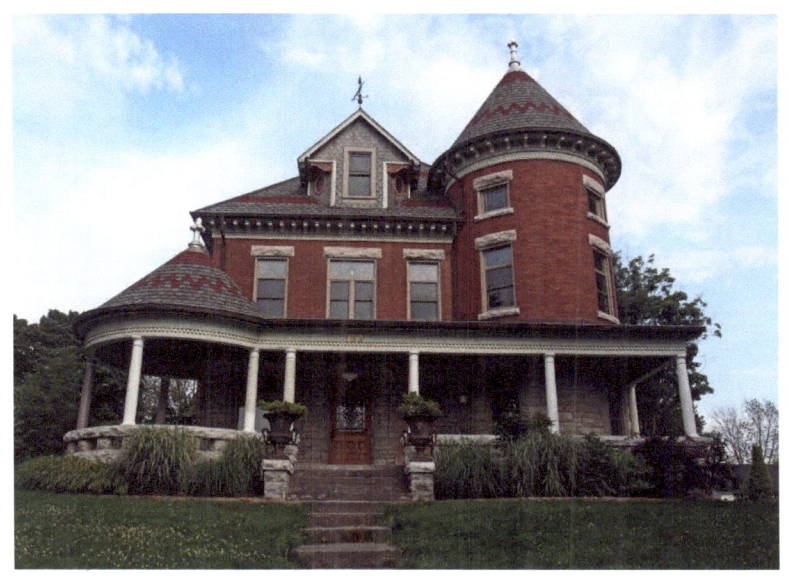

163 Church Street South – Queen Anne style, turret, dentil moulding, dichromatic tile work, wraparound verandah

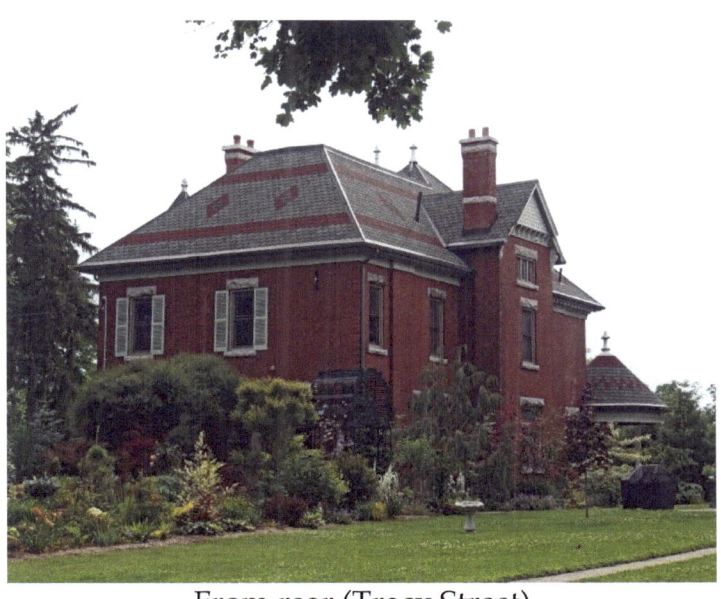

From rear (Tracy Street)

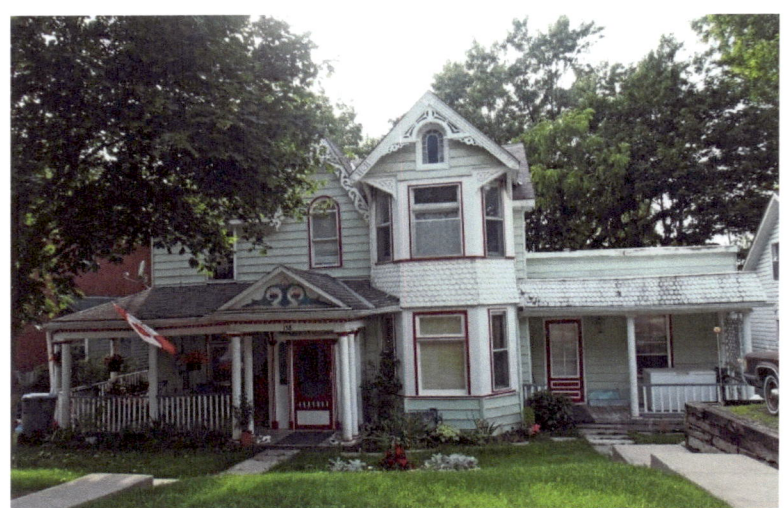

158 Church Street South – verge board trim on gable

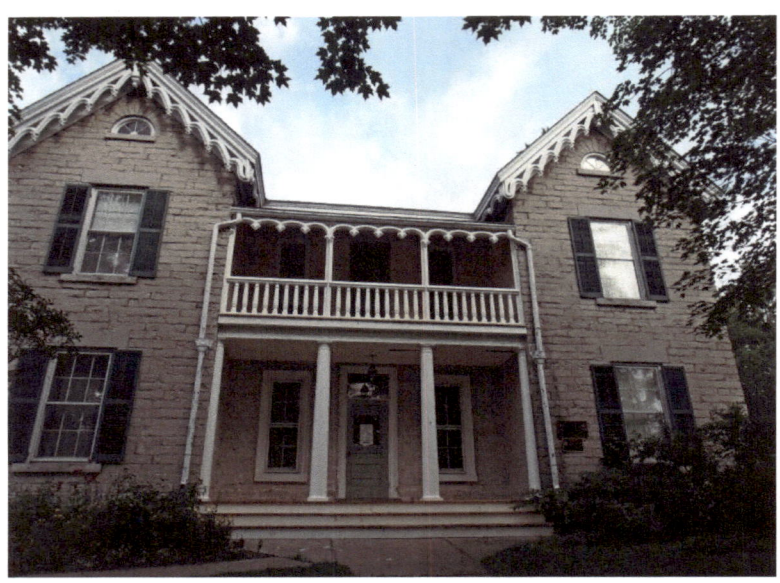

177 Church Street South – St. Marys Museum in Cadzow Park
- pillared entrance with second floor balcony

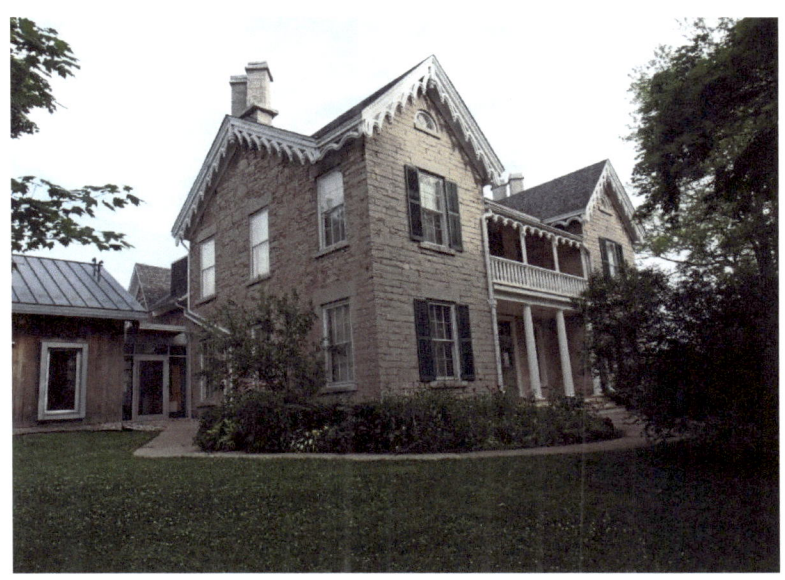

177 Church Street South – built in 1854 of local limestone for George Tracey, an early pioneer – the house was nicknamed "Castle in the Bush" - Gothic Revival, verge board trim on gables

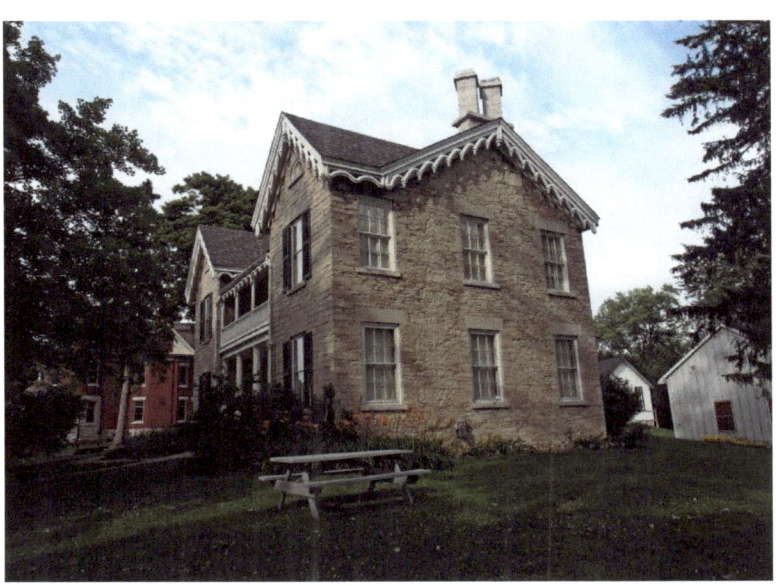

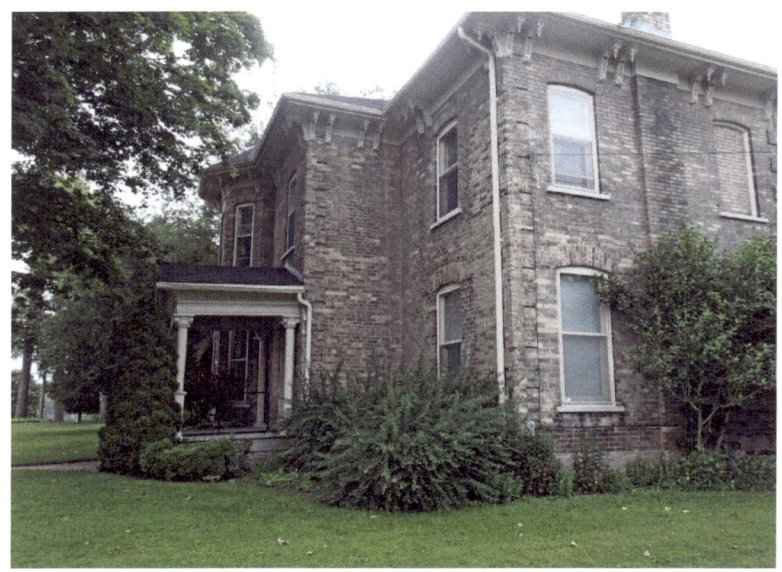

Elgin Street East – hipped roof, cornice brackets

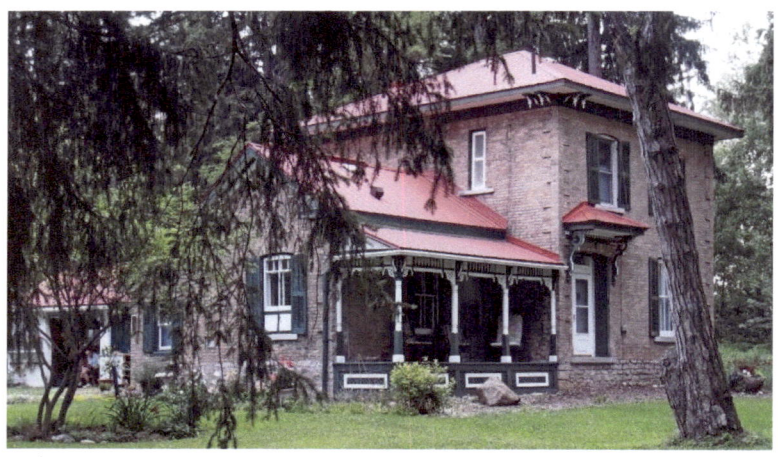

254 Elgin Street West - Meighen House, ninth prime minister of Canada – Italianate, hipped roof, cornice brackets

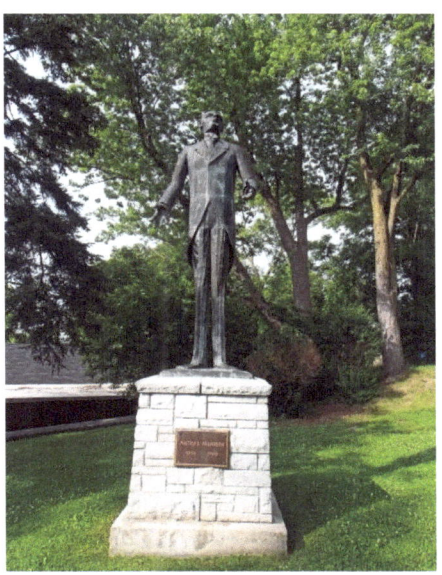

Arthur Meighen statue in Lind Park

Arthur Meighen's grandfather Gordon came to St Marys in 1843, emigrating from Londonderry, Ireland. He was the town's first school teacher and bought a farm in nearby Anderson. Gordon Meighen's son Joseph was 13 when his father died and left school to help his mother with the farm. Joseph married Mary Jane Bell and Arthur Meighen was born here in 1874, the second of six children.

The family moved to a dairy farm at the edge of St Marys in 1886; the house is at 254 Elgin St West. Arthur completed high school in St. Marys, and then enrolled at the University of Toronto. Each summer he returned to help sell his father's dairy products. After graduation, Arthur worked as a storekeeper in nearby Woodham, and then taught in Calendonia, before going to Winnipeg where he became a lawyer.

Arthur Meighen's parents remained in St. Marys at the house at 254 Elgin Street West until 1917 when they moved to 162 Church Street South. They moved to Ottawa in 1920.

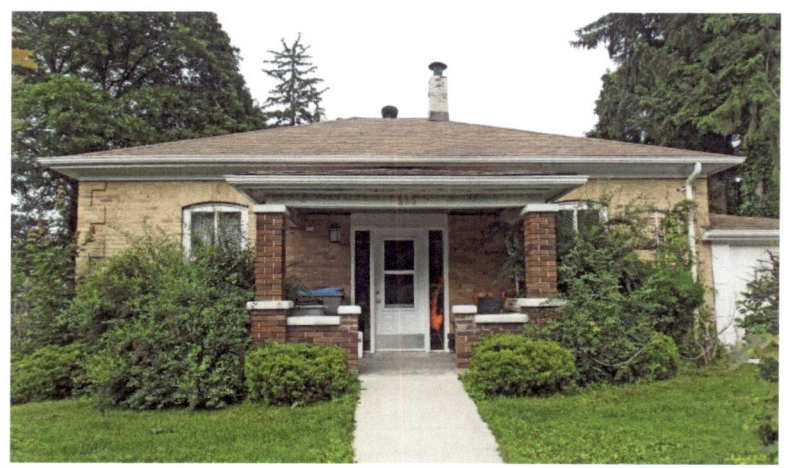

135 Elizabeth Street – Regency Cottage – corner quoins, hipped roof, single storey, sidelights around door

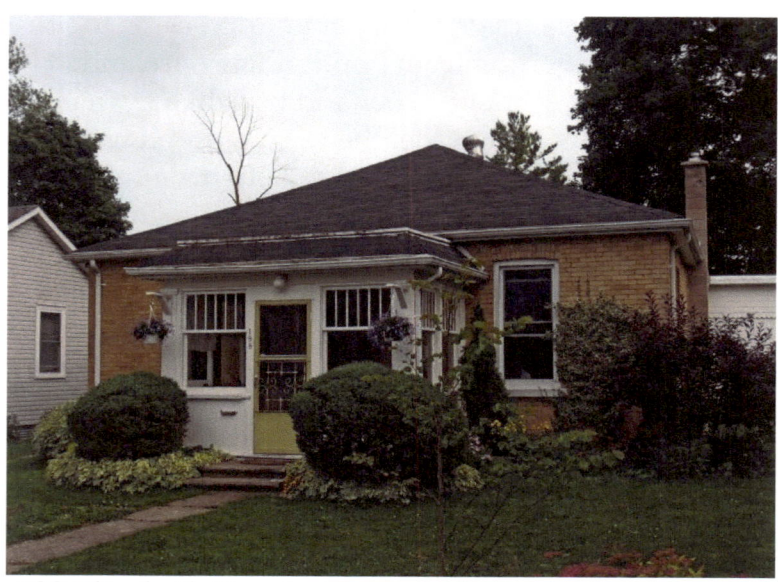

188 Elizabeth Street – Regency Cottage – hipped roof

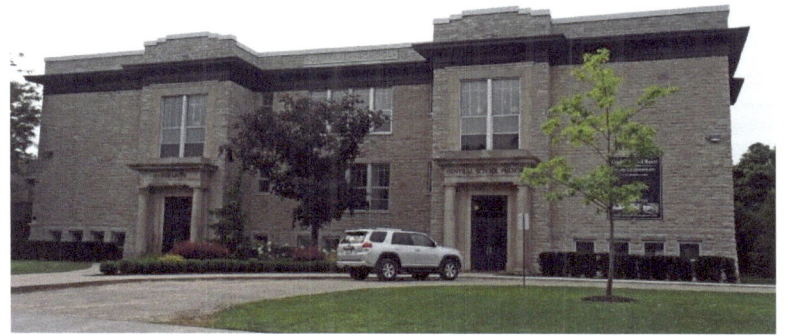

189 Elizabeth Street – Central School – Doric pillars
A.D. 1914 – now luxury condominiums

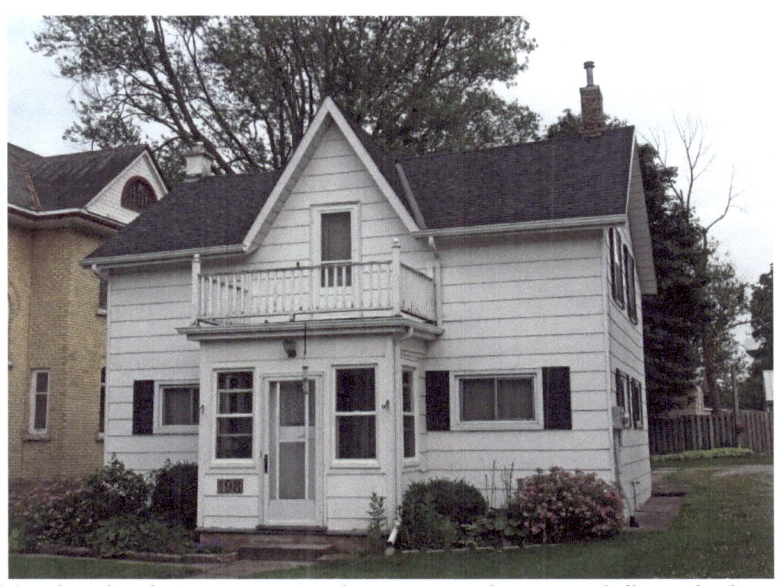

198 Elizabeth Street – Gothic Revival, second floor balcony

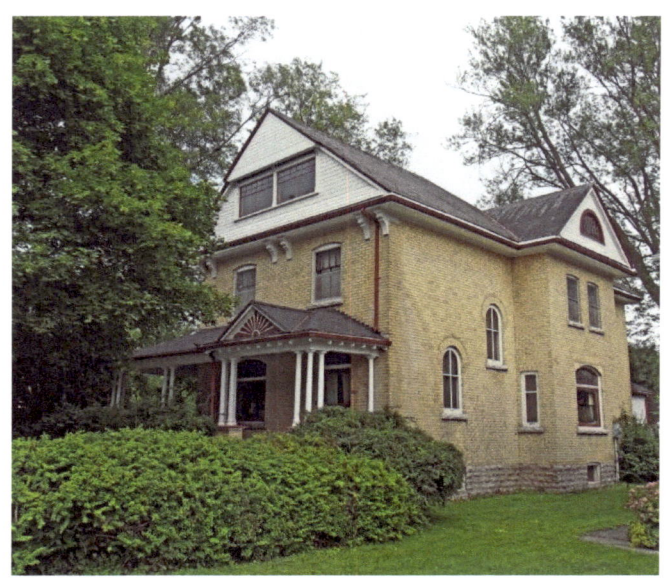

204 Elizabeth Street – cornice brackets, various shaped windows, pediment above verandah with decorated tympanum

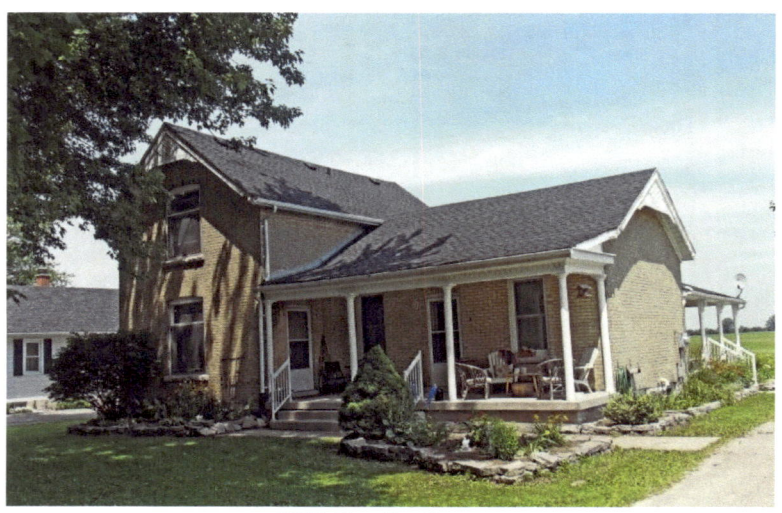

375 Emily Street

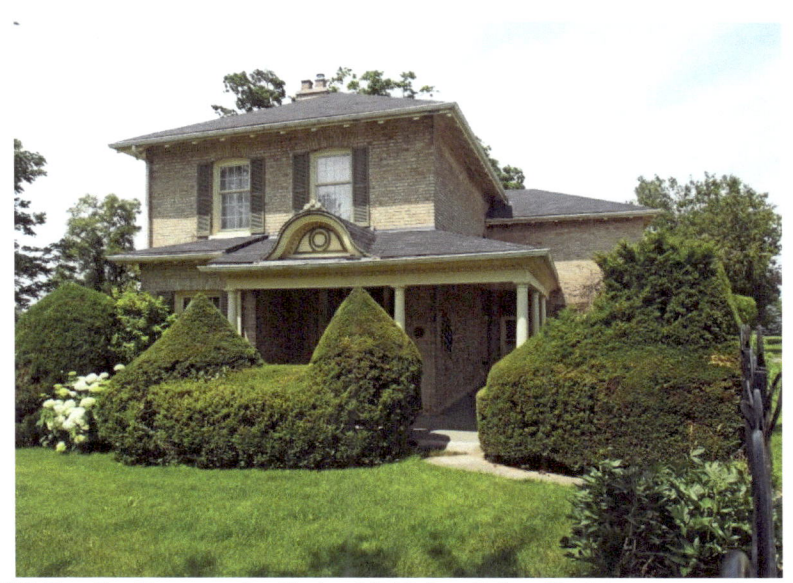

322 Emily Street - built in 1860 for John Robinson, a Grand
Trunk Railway civil engineer – Italianate, pediment with
decorated tympanum

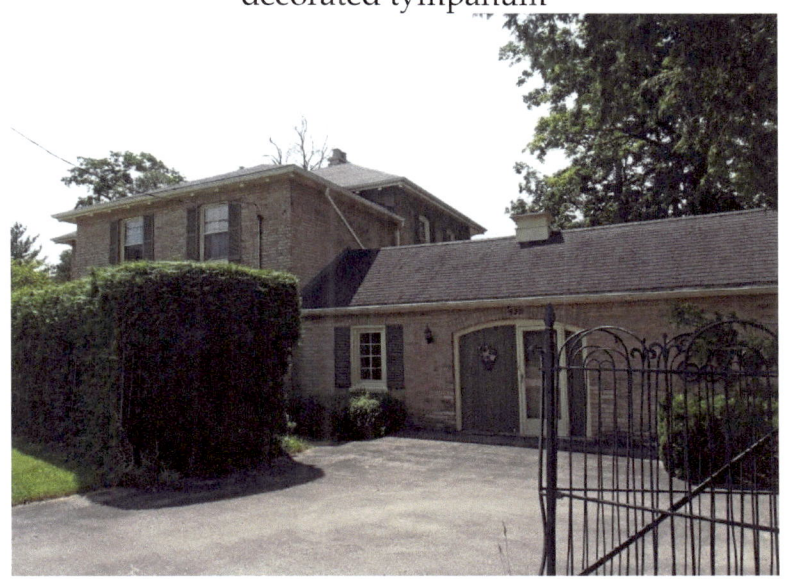

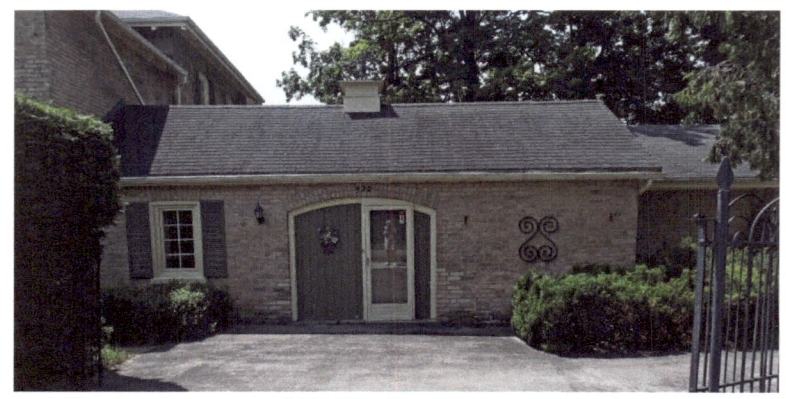

322 Emily Street
Dr. Thomas Sparks lived here before moving to 236 Jones
Street

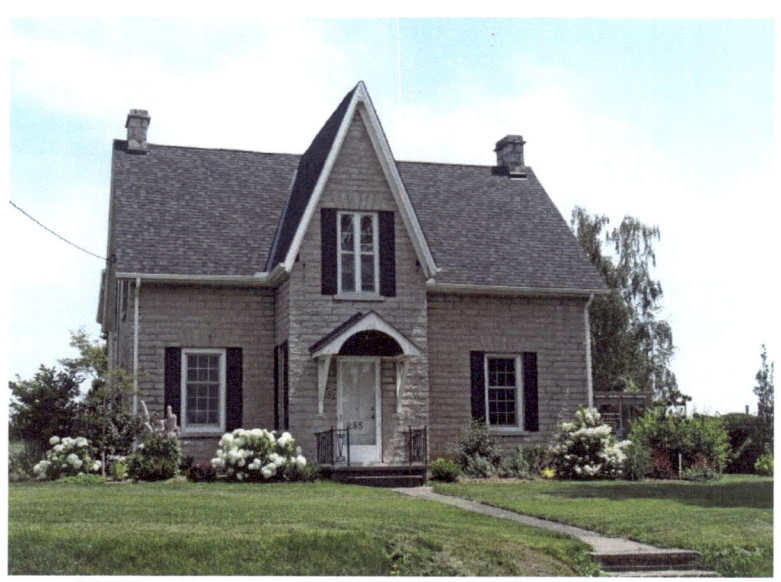

285 Emily Street – limestone 1½ storey house

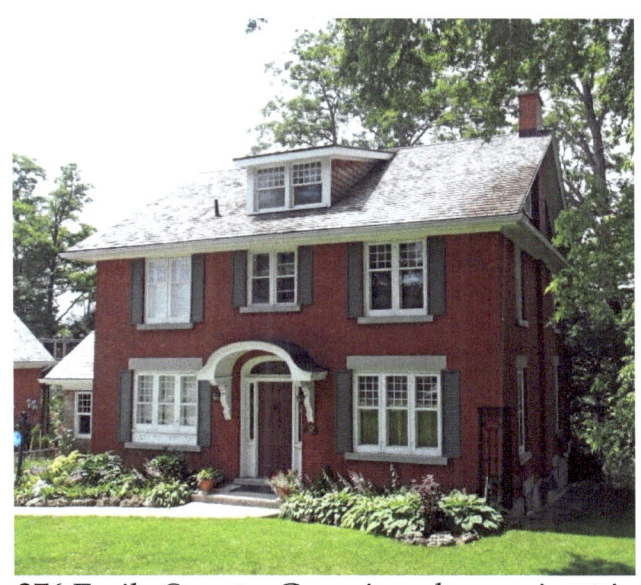

276 Emily Street – Georgian, dormer in attic

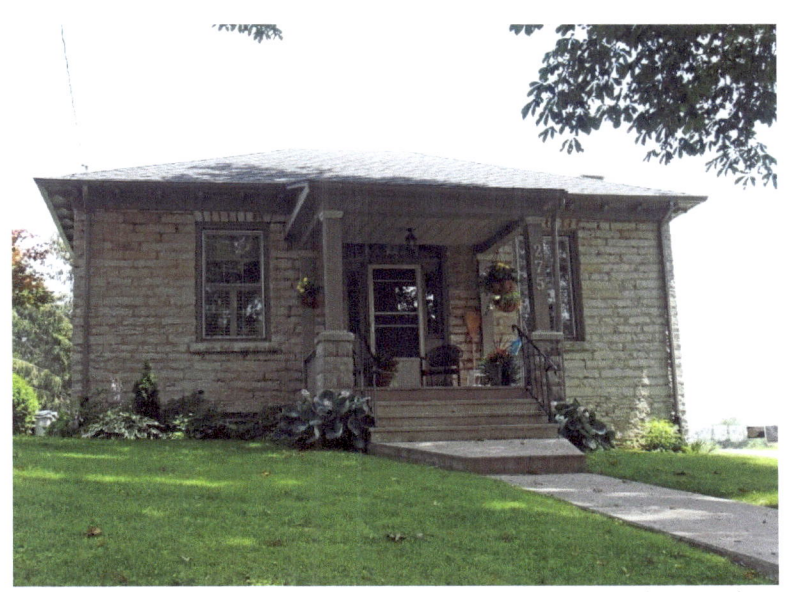

275 Emily Street – limestone Regency Cottage, hipped roof

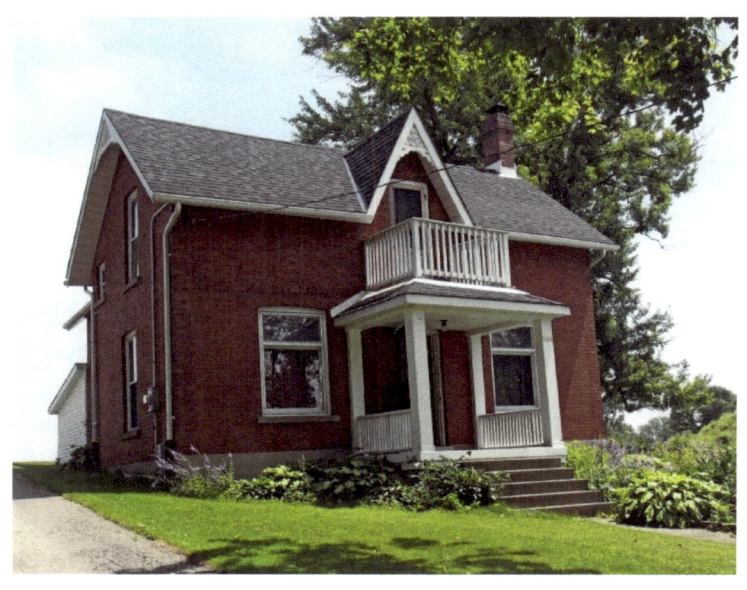

269 Emily Street – Gothic Revival – decorative trim at top of gables, second floor balcony

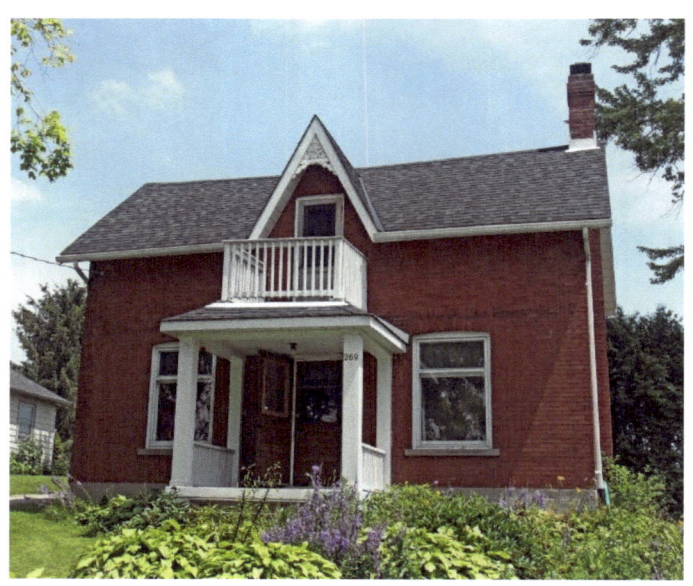

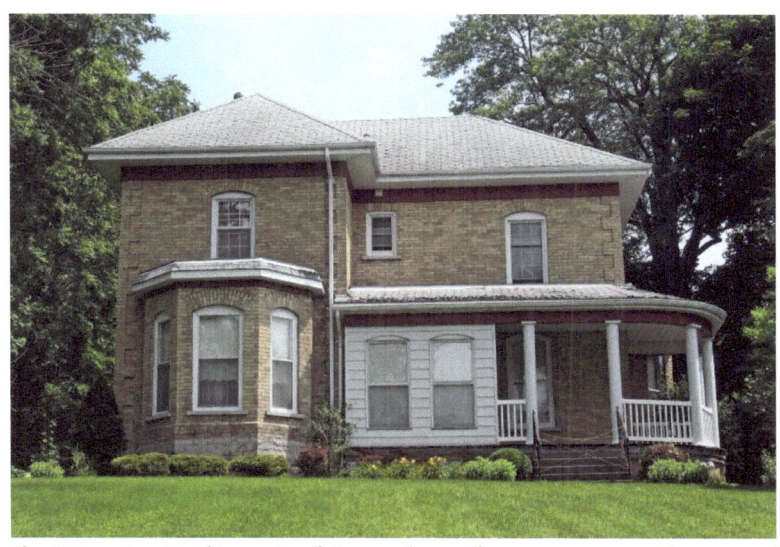

Emily Street – Italianate, hipped roof, wraparound verandah, bay window

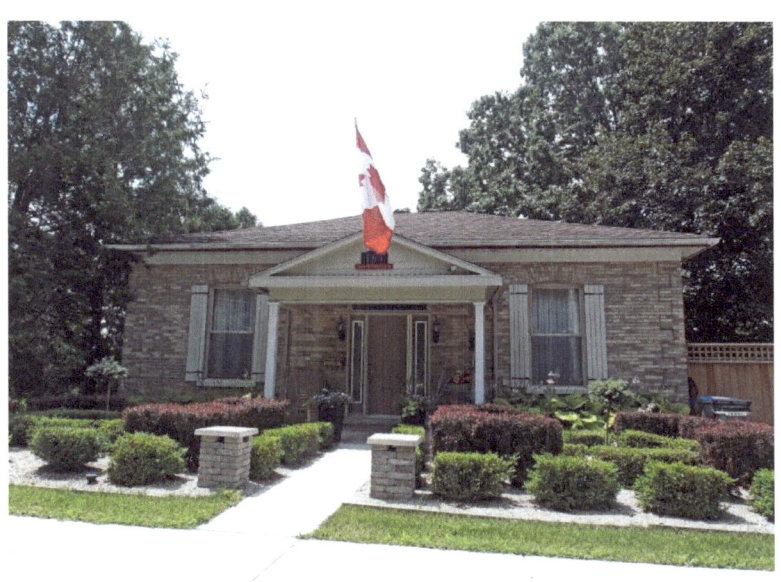

164 Emily Street – limestone Regency Cottage, pediment

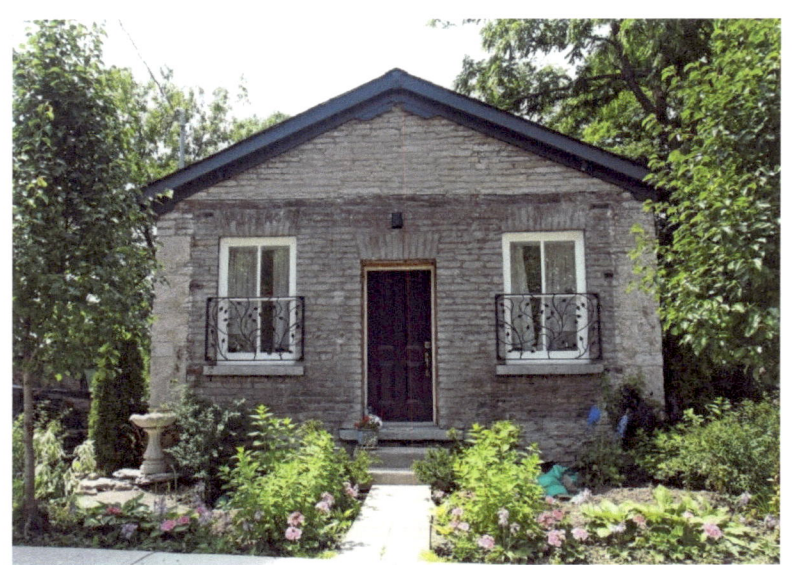

Emily Street - limestone cottage

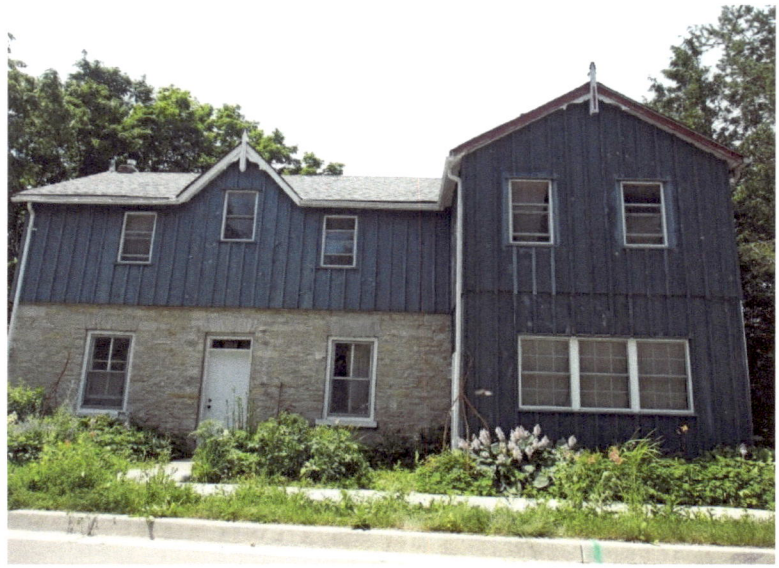

Emily Street – limestone lower level, finals on gables

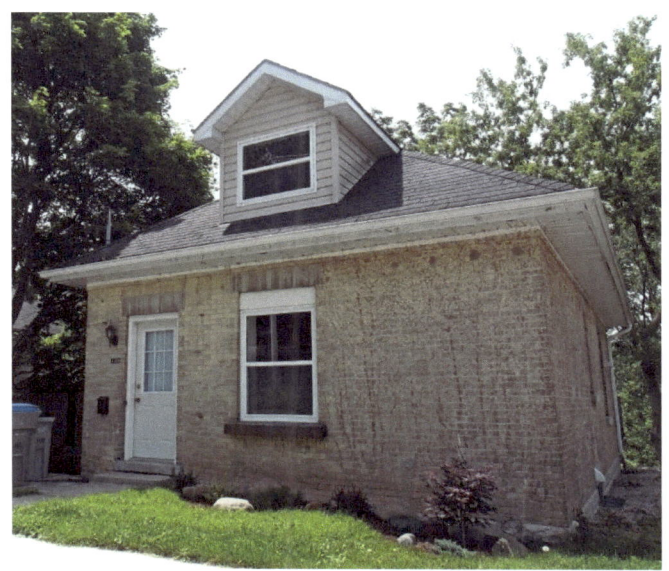

136 Emily Street – limestone, hipped roof with dormer

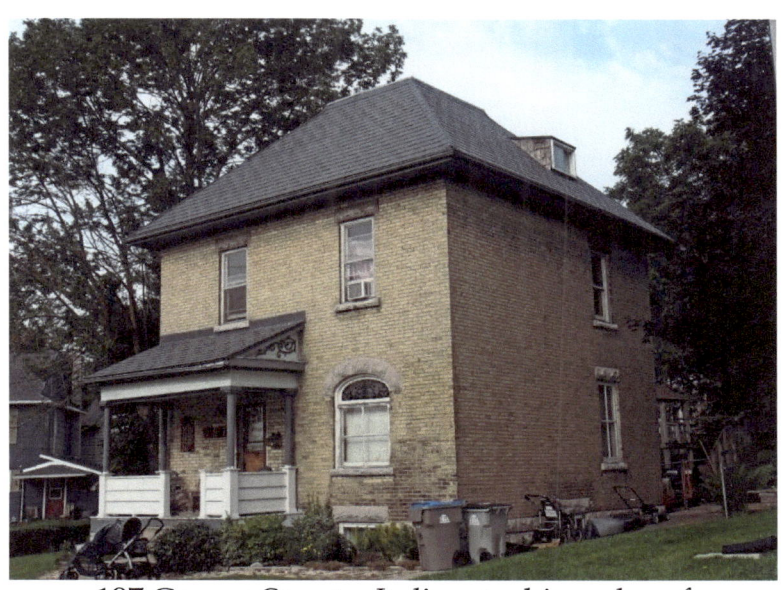

197 George Street – Italianate, hipped roof

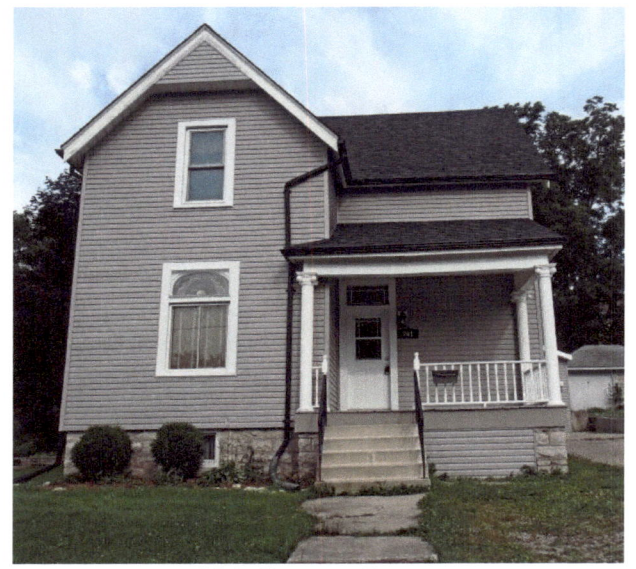

201 George Street

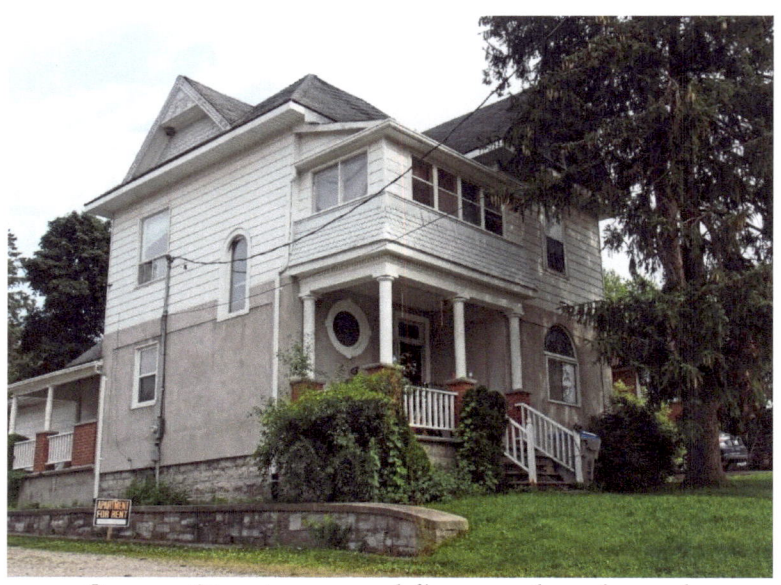

George Street – second floor enclosed porch

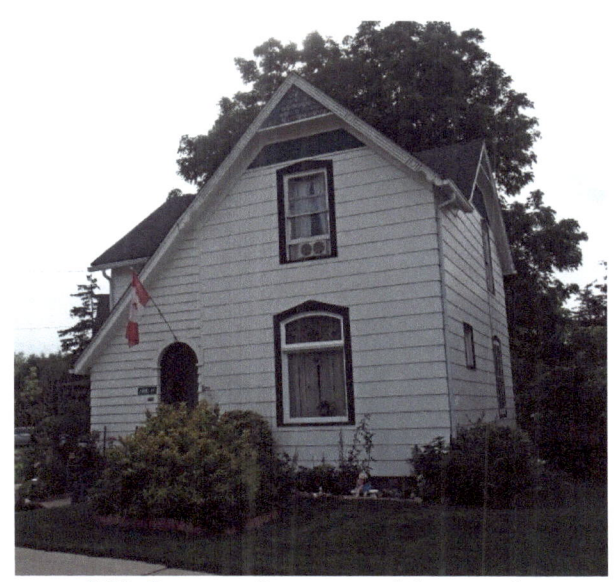

220 George Street – saltbox style

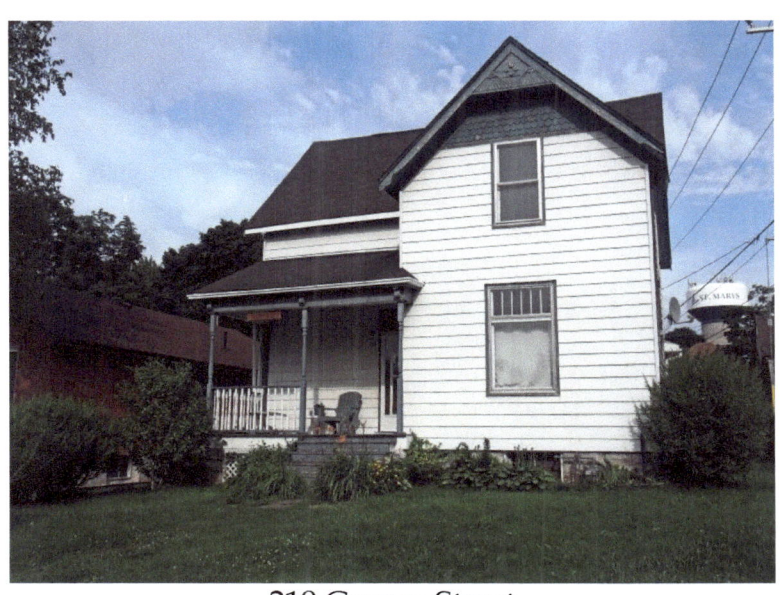

219 George Street

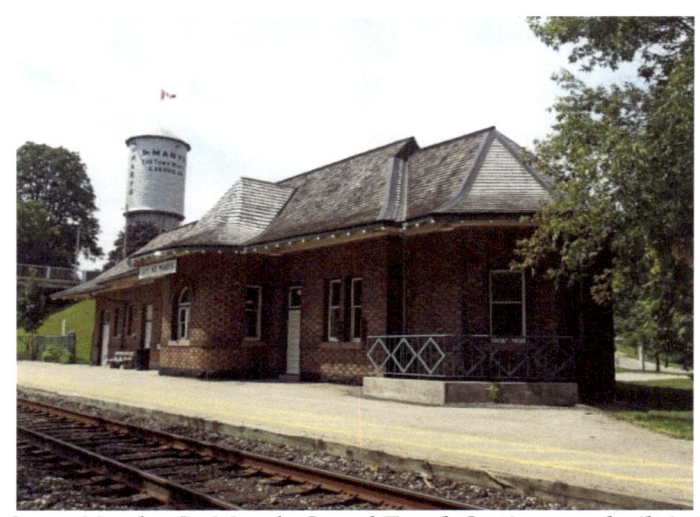

5 James Street North - St. Mary's Grand Trunk Station was built in 1907 of a glazed brick of brownish tint known as Logan Brick. Originally the depot contained a main waiting room with a ticket and operating room at the rear, men's and women's toilets, a ladies' retiring room, a smoking room for men and an express department located at the north end

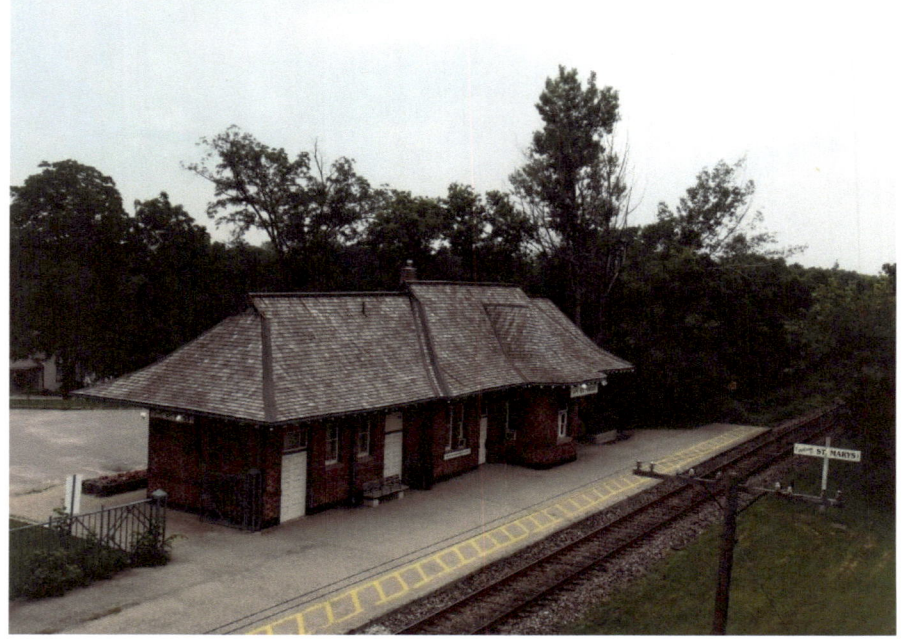

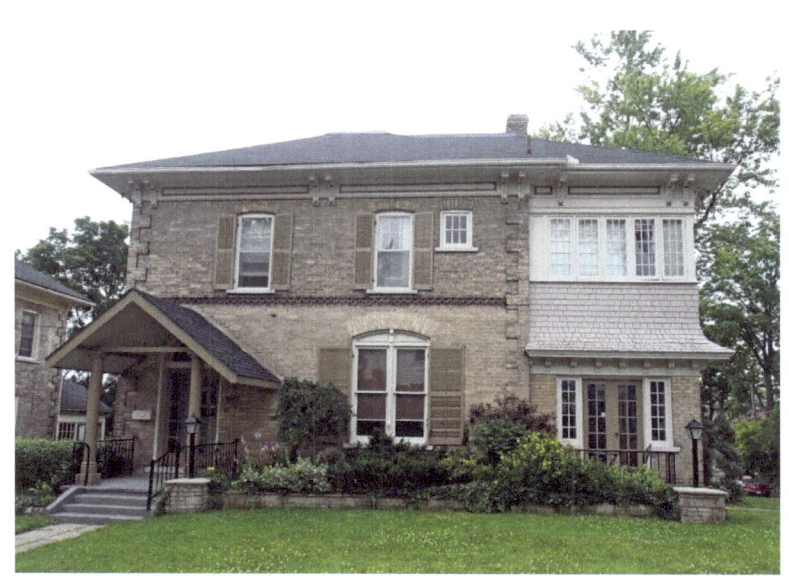

201 Jones Street East – Italianate – hipped roof, corner quoins, paired cornice brackets

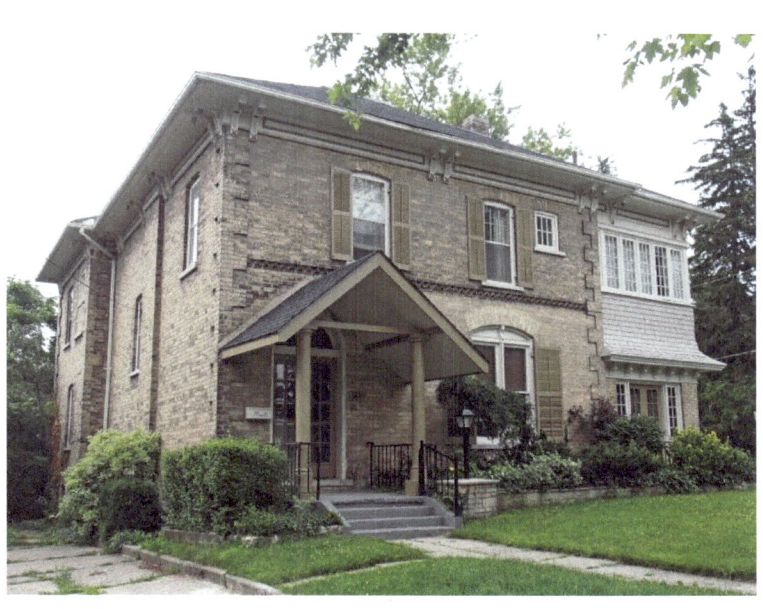

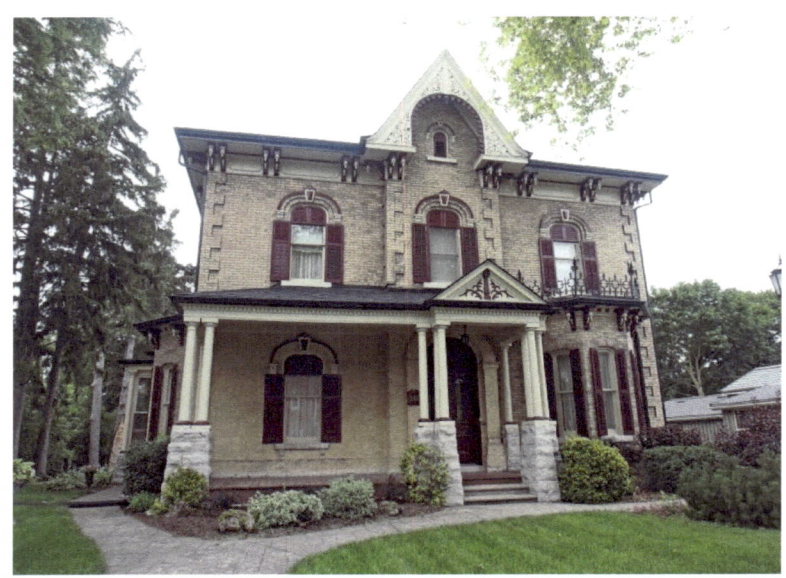

217 Jones Street East – Italianate style – 1875 – verge board trim on gable, cornice brackets, pediment with decorated tympanum, pillars with Doric capitals supporting verandah, bay window with iron cresting above, corner quoins, curved window voussoirs with keystones

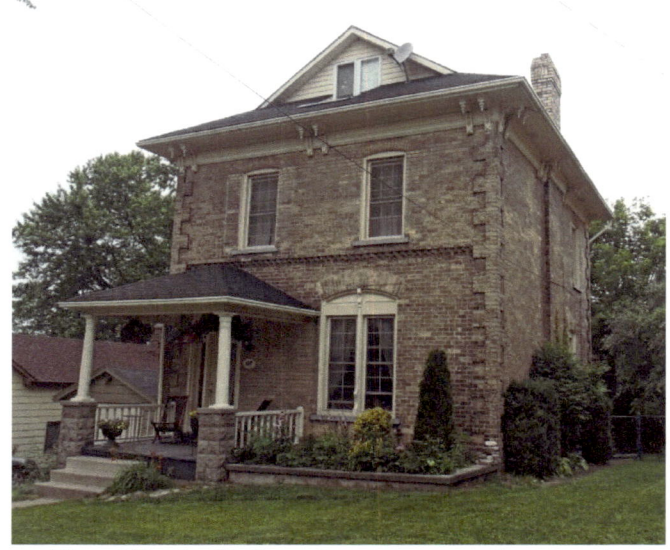

197 Jones Street East – Italianate, corner quoins, cornice brackets

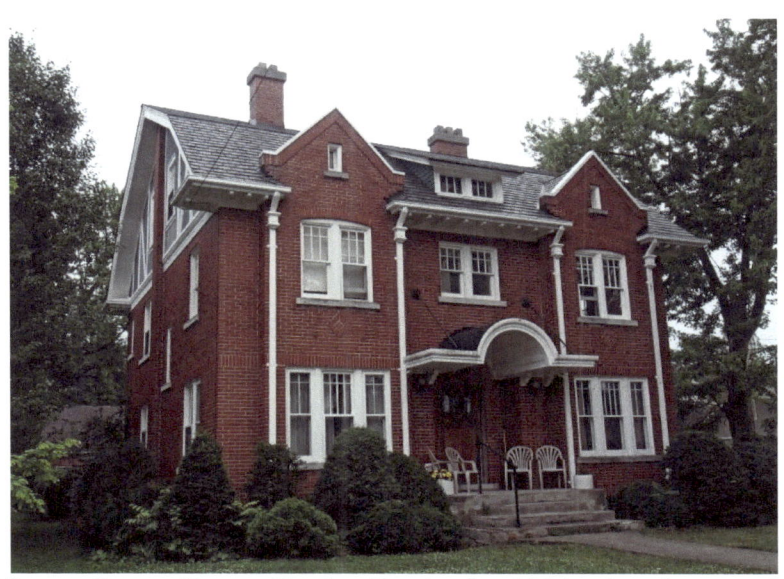

218 Jones Street East – Tudor Revival – 1914 – Jacobean gables, dormer, gambrel roof

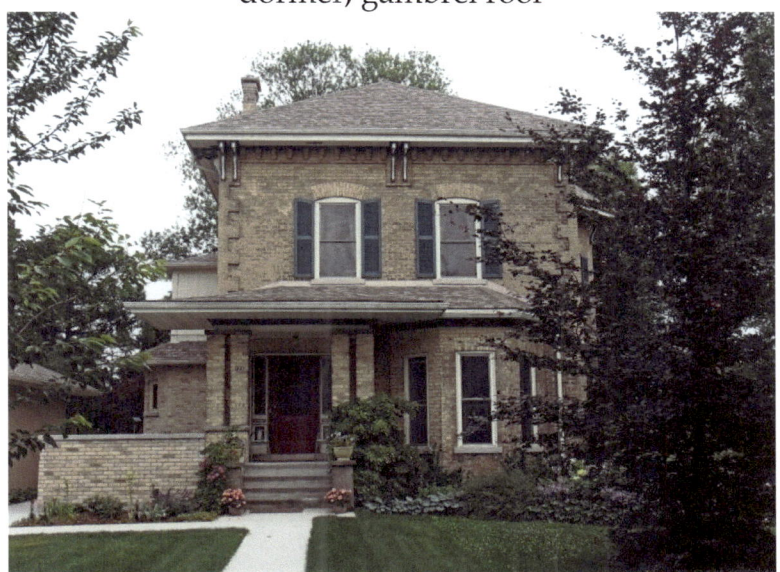

224 Jones Street East – built in 1869 for George Carter who established his grain business in St. Marys – Italianate, paired cornice brackets with smaller ones in-between, corner quoins, bay window

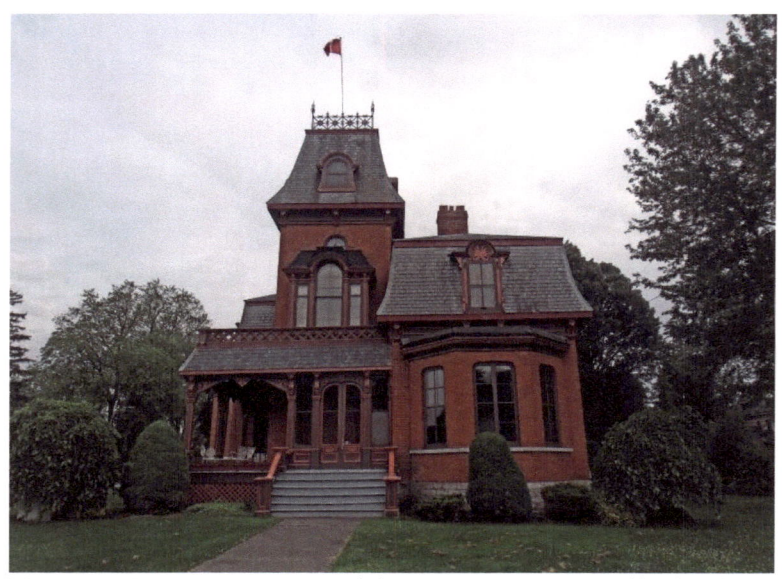

236 Jones Street East - Ercildoune was originally built as a wedding gift to George Carter's daughter Charlotte when she married Henry Lincoln Rice in 1880. The home is built in the Second Empire style, a very rare style of home in St. Marys.

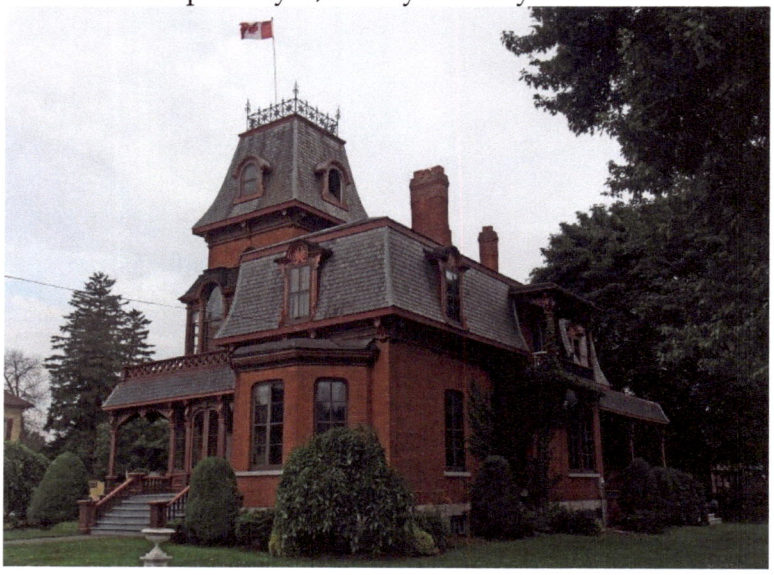

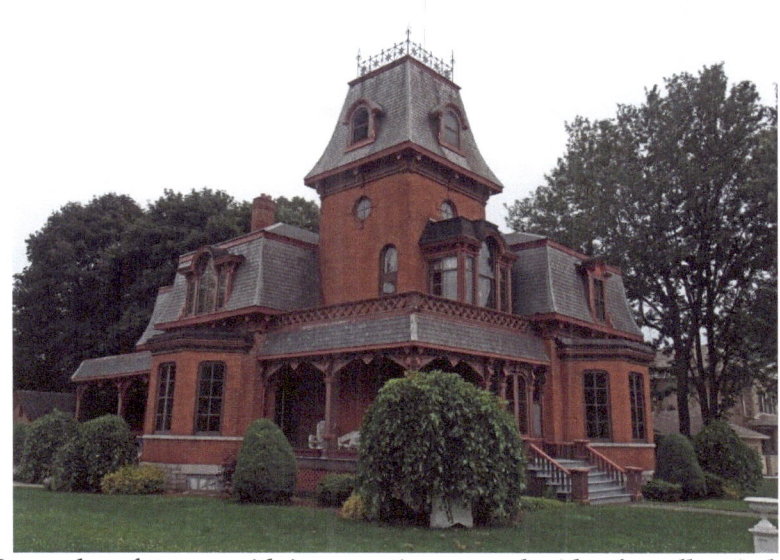

Mansard roof, tower with iron cresting around widow's walk, window
hoods, second floor balconies, wraparound gracious verandahs
The Sparks' family lived in this home from 1905 to the 1950s. St. Marys
physician and public speaker Thomas Sparks moved to the house in
1905.   He named it *Ercildoune* after his birthplace in Scotland.

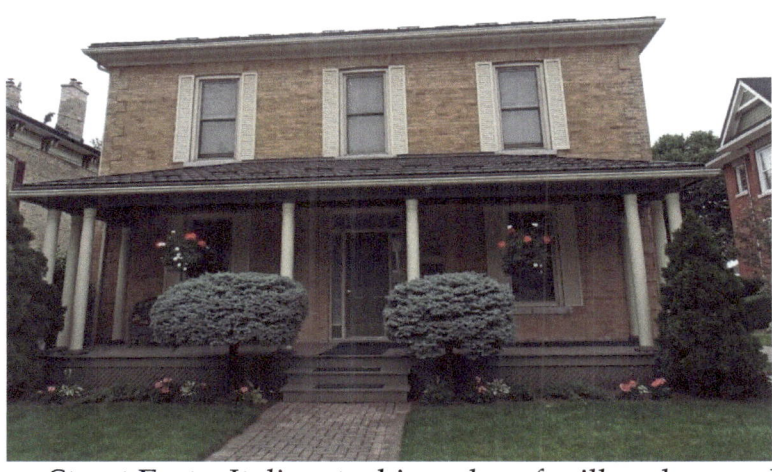

Jones Street East – Italianate, hipped roof, pillared verandah

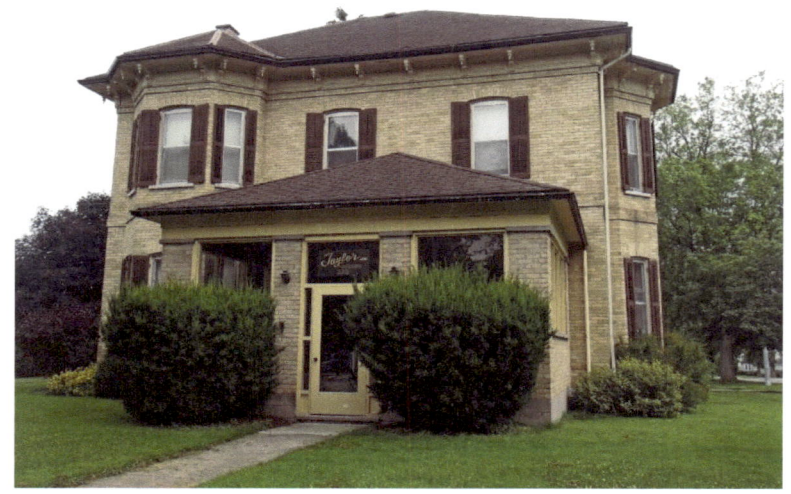

252 Jones Street East – Italianate, hipped roof, two-storey tower-like bays, cornice brackets

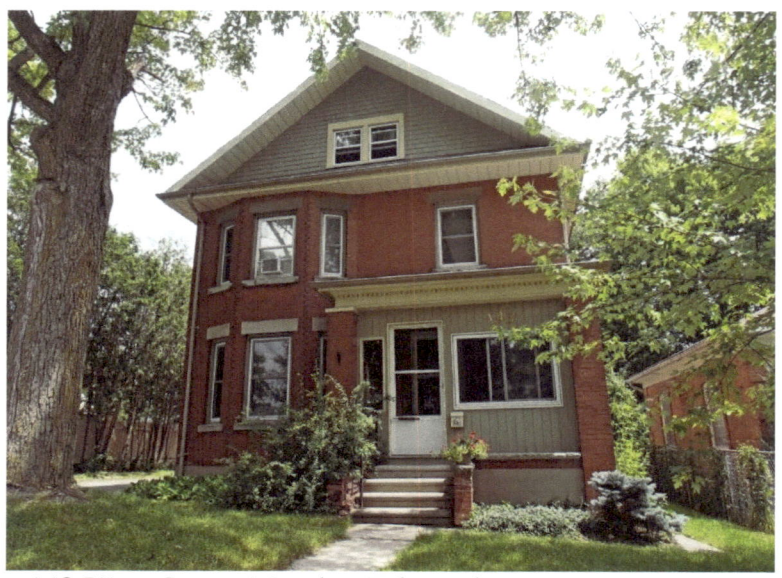

143 King Street North – Edwardian, two-storey bay

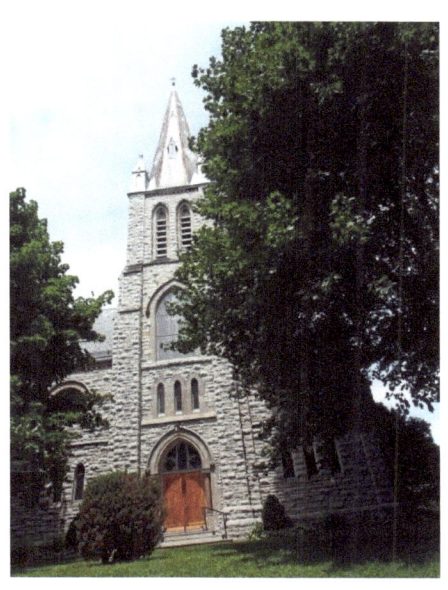

149 King Street North – Holy Name of Mary Catholic Church – 1892 – Gothic Revival style – buttresses, lancet windows, dichromatic tilework on roof – 69-foot central tower topped by a 61-foot steeple

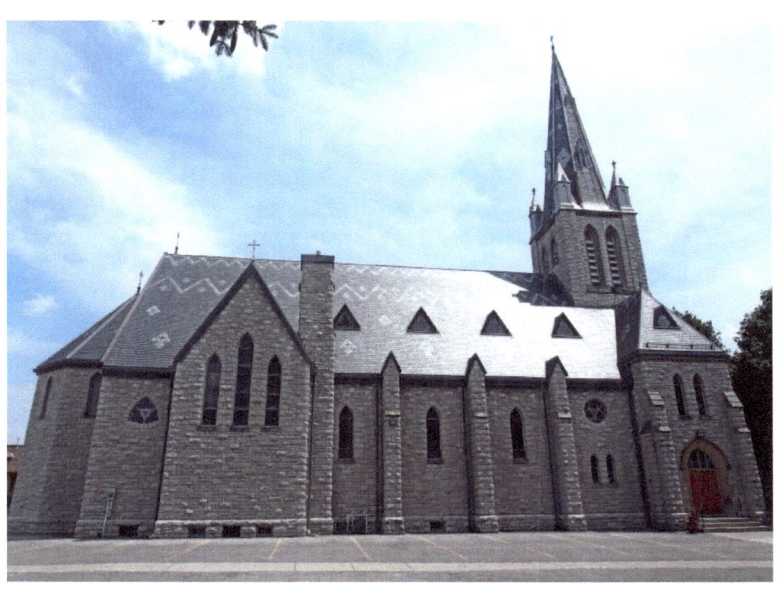

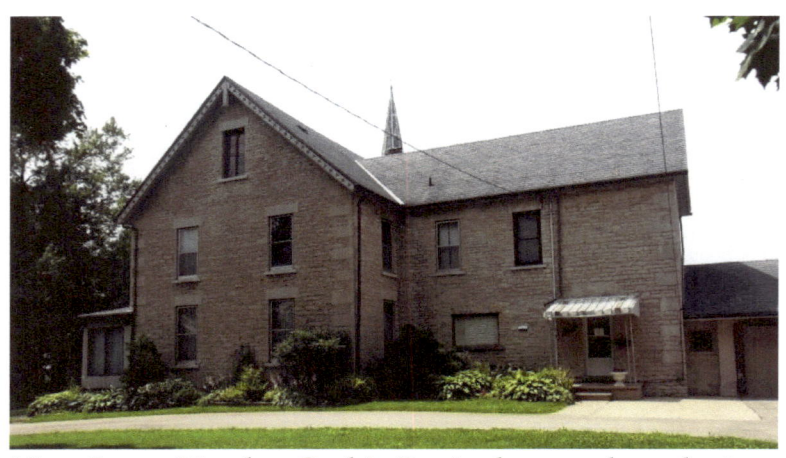

149 King Street North – Gothic Revival, verge board trim with finial on gable, corner quoins

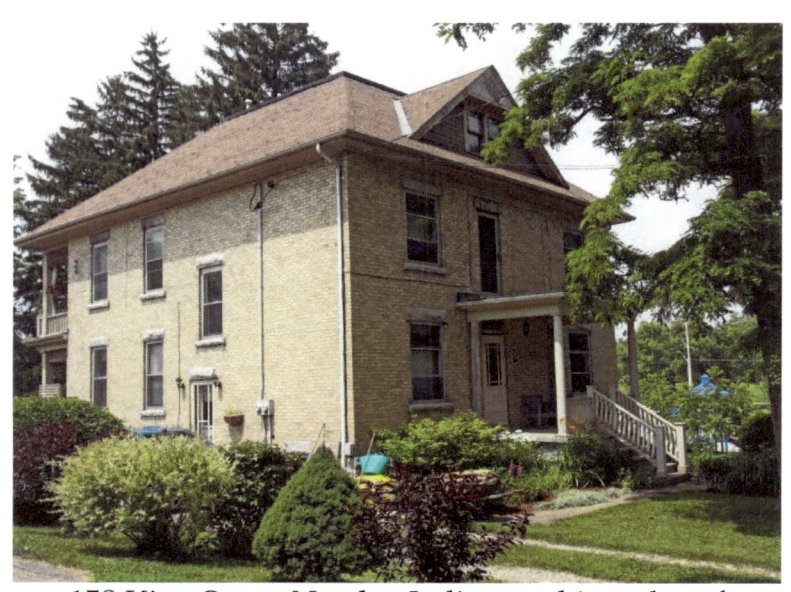

158 King Street North – Italianate, hipped roof

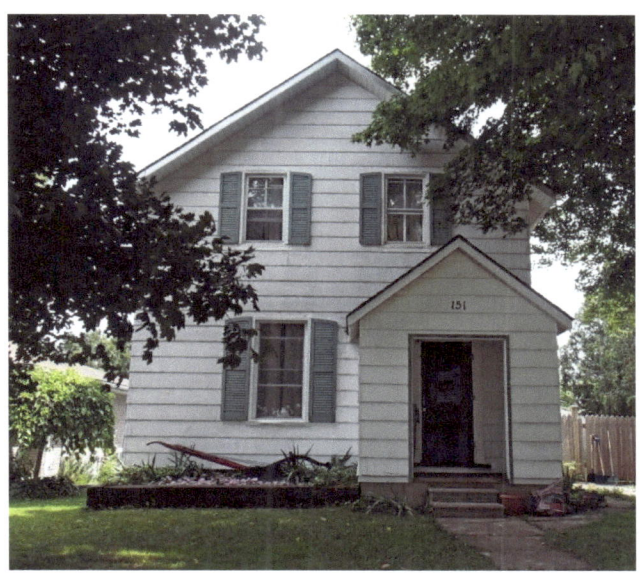

151 King Street North

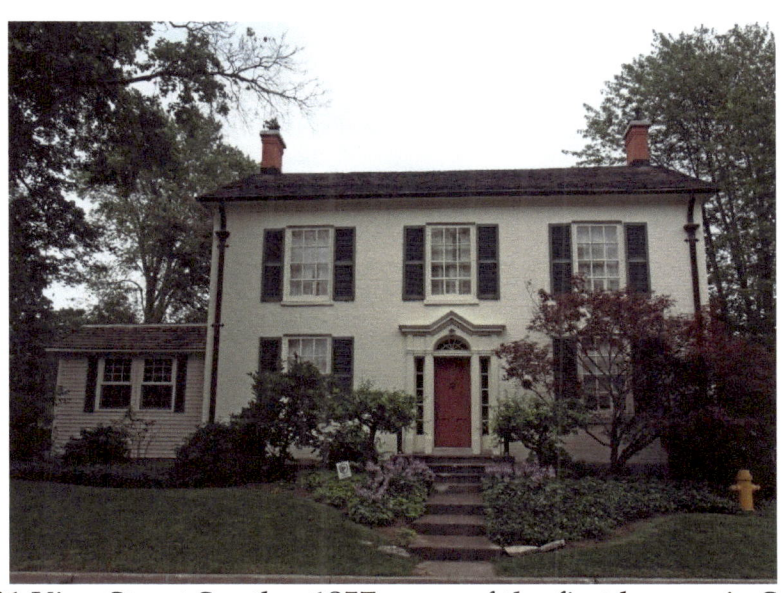

31 King Street South – 1857 – one of the first houses in St. Marys built of brick (salmon-pink now painted white) – Classical Revival

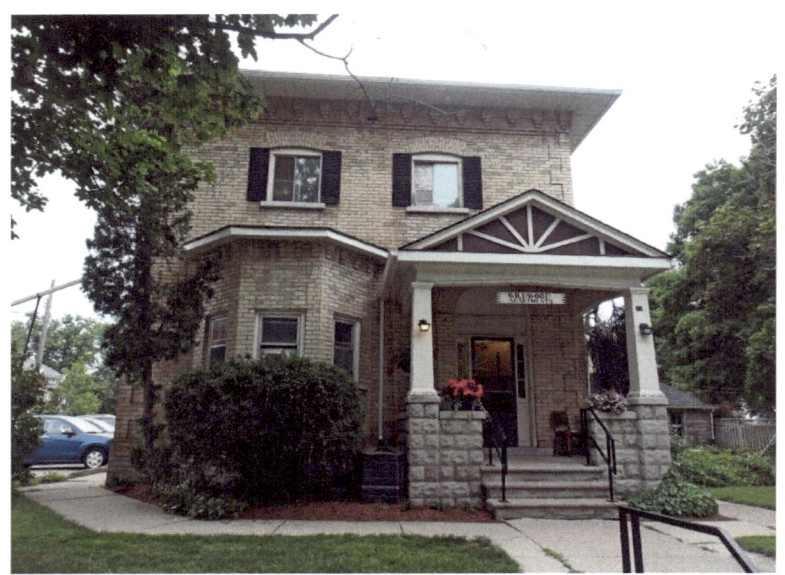

32 King Street South – Italianate, hipped roof, bay window, pediment with decorated tympanum

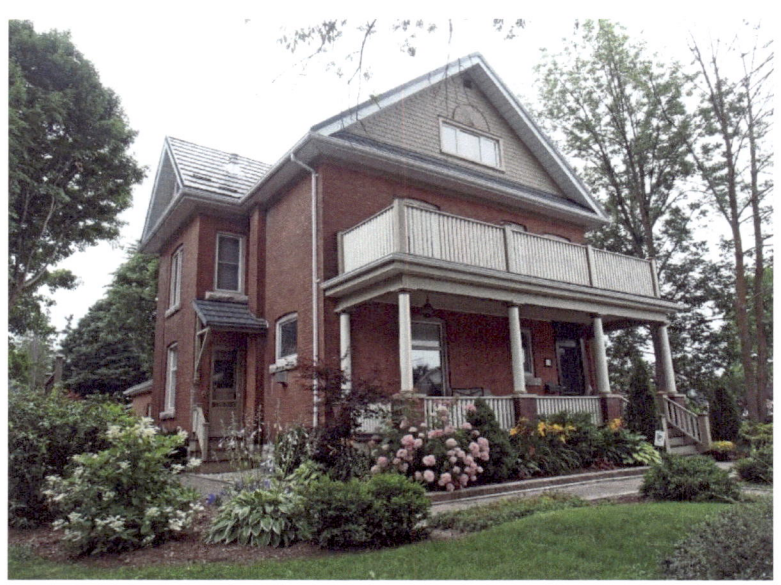

24 King Street South – Edwardian, two-storey verandah

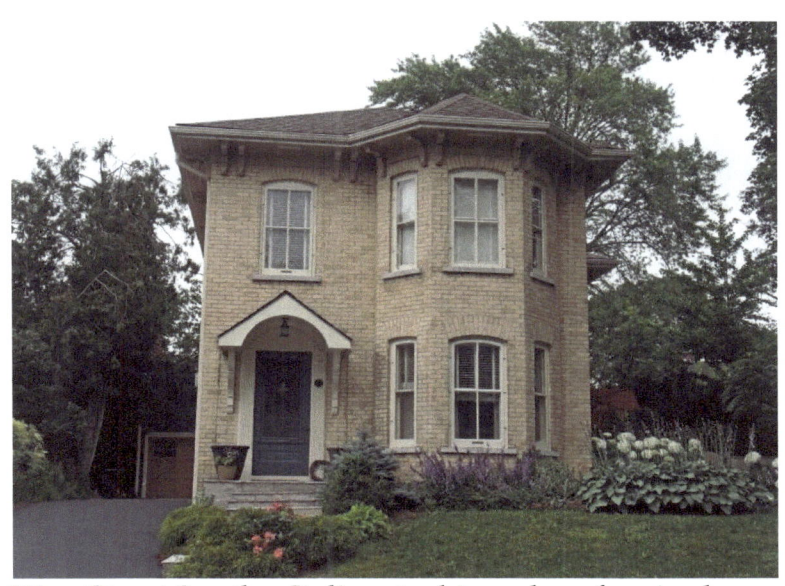

21 King Street South – Italianate, hipped roof, paired cornice brackets, two-storey bay window

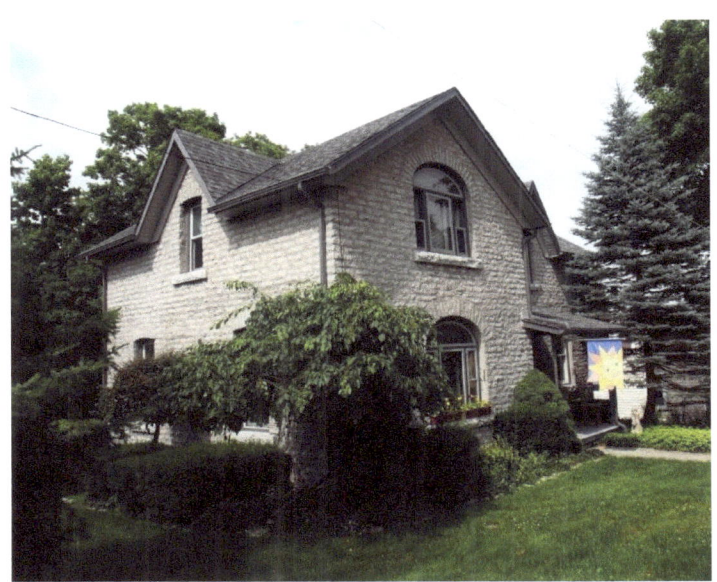

163 Maiden Lane – limestone – Gothic Revival

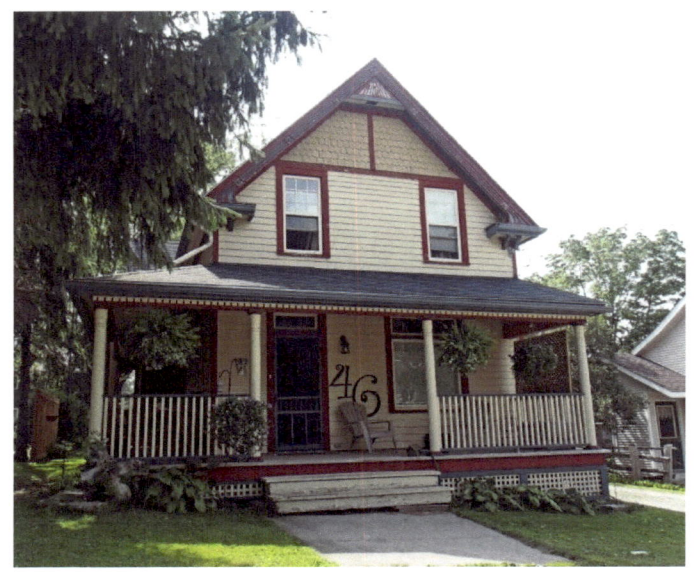

46 Maiden Lane

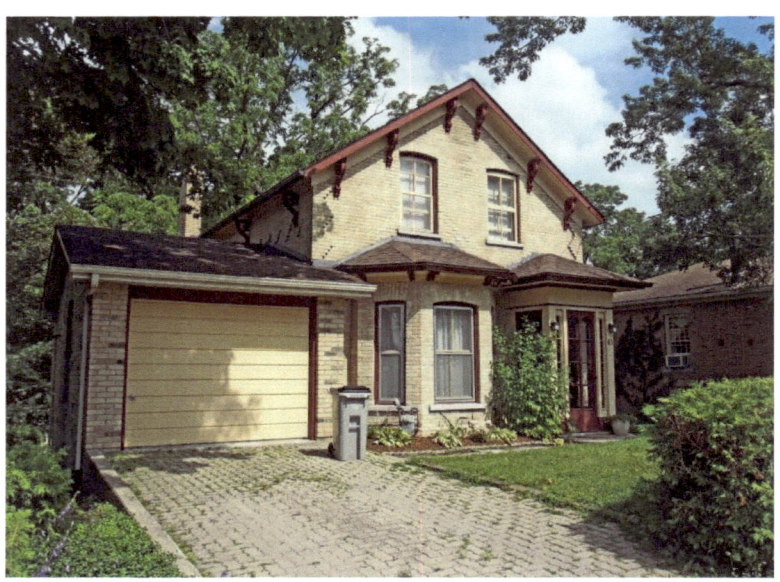

41 Maiden Lane – cornice brackets, bay window

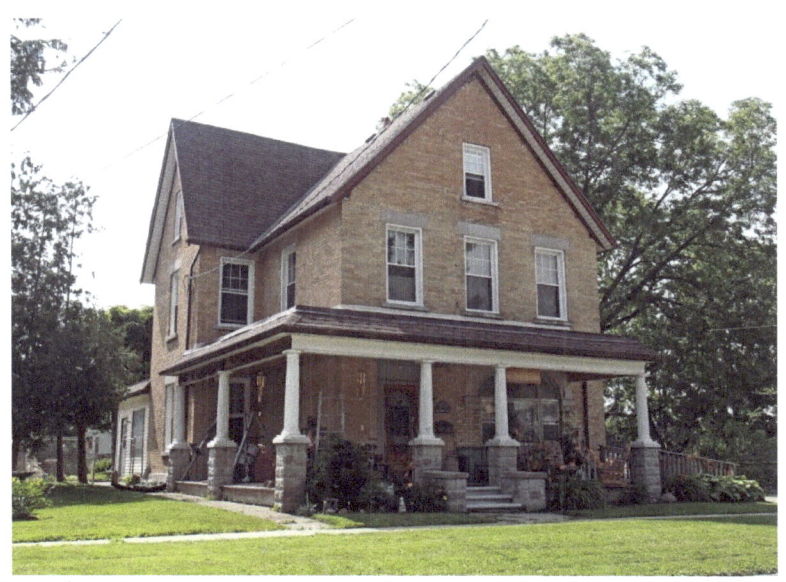

Maiden Lane – wraparound verandah with Doric pillars

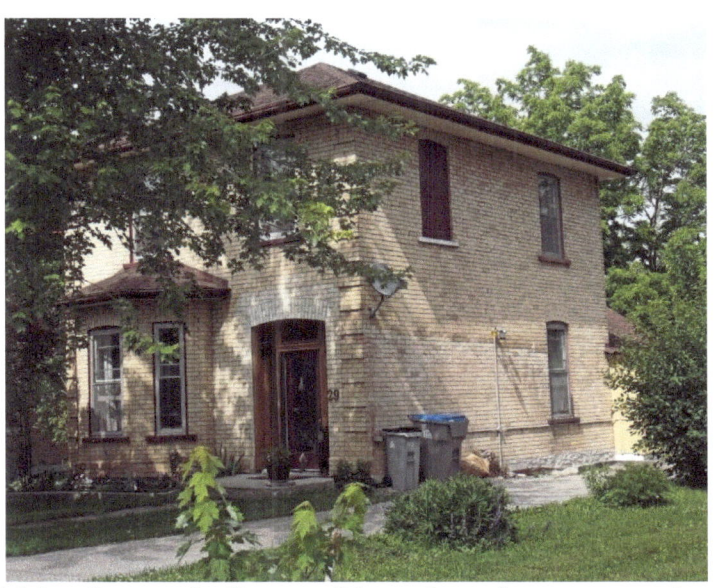

29 Maiden Lane – Italianate, hipped roof, corner quoins, bay window

Architectural Terms

Bay Window: A window that projects out from a wall, in a semicircular, rectangular, or polygonal design. Used frequently in Gothic and Victorian designs. Example: Emily Street, Page 35	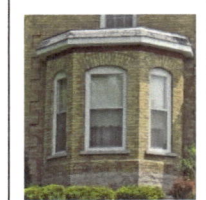
Brackets: a decorative or weight-bearing structural element which forms a right angle with one side against a wall and the other under a projecting surface such as an eave or roof. Example: Elgin Street East, Page 26	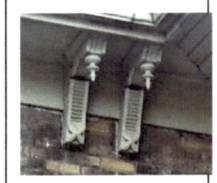
Buttress: a masonry structure built against or projecting from a wall which serves to support or reinforce the wall. In Canadian architecture, they are sometimes used for decoration. Example: 85 Church Street South, Page 19	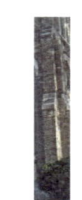
Capital: The uppermost finish or decoration on a column. A Doric column is characterized by a plain column with no base, a shaft with twenty flutings, and a simple capital with a simple entablature. A Corinthian column is characterized by a rounded capital decorated with acanthus leaves and a square abacus (the uppermost portion of a capital directly below the entablature) on tall slender columns. Example: Corinthian: 15 Church Street North, Page 12; Doric: Maiden Lane, Page 53	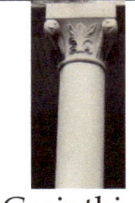 Corinthian 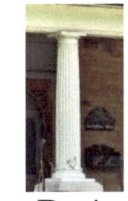 Doric

Cobblestone architecture: Refers to the use of cobblestones embedded in mortar as a method for erecting walls on houses and commercial buildings. Example: 98 Church Street North, Page 10	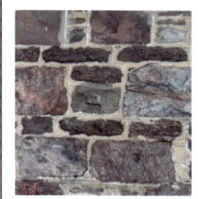
Cornice: originally the wooden overhang of the roof. With the use of stone, brick, iron and steel, the cornice is any projecting shelf at the top of a ceiling or roof. They can be very decorative. Example: 46 Church Street South, Page 17	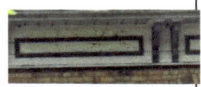
Dentil Moulding: an even series of rectangles used as ornamental decoration in cornices. Example: 85 Church Street South, Page 19	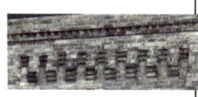
Dichromatic brickwork: the use of two colours of brick, tile or slate to decorate a façade. Example: 163 Church Street, Page 23	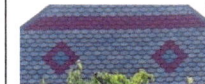
Dormer: (French for "sleep") a gable end window that pierces through the plane of a sloping roof surface to create usable space in the top floor or attic of a building by adding headroom. Example: 136 Emily Street, Page 37	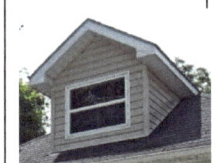
Entrance: The entrance encompasses the doorway and the inner vestibule or, in residential architecture, the covered porch. Example: 46 Church Street, Page 17	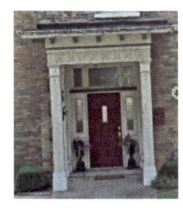

Gable: the triangular portion of a wall between the edges of a sloping roof. **Jacobean Gable:** the gable extends above the roofline. Example: 218 Jones Street East, Page 43	
Gambrel Roof: a symmetrical two-sided roof with two slopes on each side; the upper slope is positioned at a shallow angle, while the lower slope is steep. It is similar to a mansard roof, but a gambrel has vertical gable ends instead of being hipped at the four corners of the building. Example: 100 Church Street North, Page 10	
Hipped Roof: a roof where all sides slope downwards to the walls with no gables. Example: 158 King Street North, Page 48	
Iron Cresting: A decorative ornament along the top of a roof. Iron cresting was popular in the Baroque era and also in Italianate, Victorian, Second Empire and Queen Anne styles of architecture. Example: 236 Jones Street East, Page 44	
Keystones and Voussoirs: a voussoir is a wedge-shaped element used in building an arch. A keystone is the central stone that locks all the stones into position, allowing the arch to bear weight. A keystone is often enlarged and embellished. Example: 217 Jones Street East, Page 42	
Lancet Window: a tall, narrow window with a pointed arch at its top. Example: 149 King Street North, Page 47	

Mansard Roof: This style was popularized by Francois Mansart (1598-1666), an accomplished architect of the French Baroque period and especially fashionable during the Second French Empire (1852-1870). This roof is almost flat on the top section, with two slopes on each of its sides with the lower slope at a steeper angle than the upper and having dormer windows. Example: 18 Church Street South, Page 14	
Pediment: a triangular section above the horizontal structure (entablature), typically supported by columns. The inside of the triangle is called the tympanum. Example: 112 Church Street North, Page 9	
Quoin: masonry blocks at the corner of a wall, often a decorative feature, usually larger or of a different colour than the rest of the wall. Example: 164 Church Street North, Page 8	
Sidelight: a window, usually with a vertical emphasis, that flanks a door, and is often used to emphasize the importance of a primary entrance. Example: 135 Elizabeth Street, Page 28	
Transom Window: the light above the doorway, also called a fanlight. Example: 276 Emily Street, Page 33	

Turret: a small tower that projects from the wall of a building. Example: 163 Church Street South, Page 23	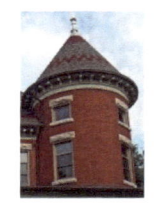
Vergeboard and Finial: also called bargeboards – hang from the projecting end of a roof and are often elaborately carved and ornamented. **Finial:** ornament added to the top of a gable, pinnacle, canopy or spire – a Gothic element. Example: 158 Church Street South, Page 24	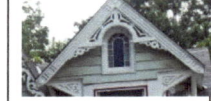
Window Hood: A **hood** is the piece found above window openings, usually of an ornate design, and covers the top third of the opening. Hoods are commonly placed above arched or curved openings on both windows and doors. Example: 236 Jones Street East, Page 45	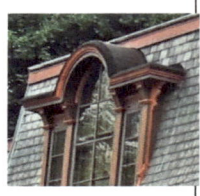

Building Styles

Beaux Arts: Promoters of this style sought to express the classical principles on a grand and imposing scale. Many of the Beaux Arts buildings were banks, post offices, and railway stations. The Ontario Beaux Arts style is eclectic mixing elements of Classical, Renaissance and Baroque. Often the designs have a temple-like façade, pedimented porticos, balustrades, capitals in many styles. Example: 15 Church Street North, Page 12	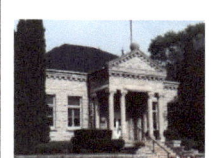
Classical Revival (1820 - 1860) – This style was an analytical, scientific, and dogmatic revival based on intensive studies of Greek and Roman buildings, concerned with the application of Greek plans and proportions to civic buildings. Schools, libraries, government offices, and most other civic buildings were built in the Classical Revival style. The white columned porches of the Classical Revival domestic buildings are identified with the mansions of wealthy land owners in Canada. Example: 31 King Street South, Page 49	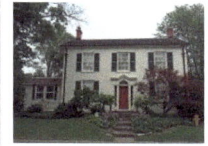
Edwardian, 1900-1930 – This style bridges the ornate and elaborate styles of the Victorian era and the simplified styles of the 20th century. Balanced facades, simple roof lines, dormer windows, large front porches, and smooth brick surfaces are its characteristics. Example: 143 King Street North, Page 46	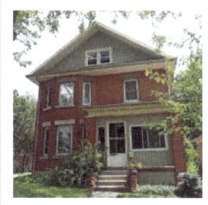

Georgian, before 1860 – This style began with the British King Georges in the 18th century. These buildings have balanced facades around a central door, medium-pitched gable roofs, and small paned windows. Example: 276 Emily Street, Page 43	
Gothic Revival, 1830-1890 – These decorative buildings have sharply-pitched gables with highly detailed verge boards, pointed-arch window openings, and dichromatic brickwork. It is a common style in Ontario. Example: 145 Church Street North, Page 7	
Italianate, 1850-1900 – It has wide-bracketed eaves, belvederes, wrap-around verandahs. Example: 217 Jones Street East, Page 42	
Queen Anne, 1885-1900 – This style is distinguished by an irregular outline featuring a combination of an offset tower, broad gables, projecting two-storey bays, verandahs, multi-sloped roofs, and tall, decorative chimneys. A mixture of brick and wood is common. Windows often have one large single-paned bottom sash and small panes in the upper sash. Example: 163 Church Street South, Page 23	
Regency Cottage, 1830-1860 – This style originated in England in 1815 and spread to Ontario later in the 19th century as British officers retired to Canada. It is a modest one-storey house with a low-pitched hip roof and has a symmetrical front façade. Example: 275 Emily Street, Page 33	

Romanesque Revival, 1880-1910 – This style hearkens back to medieval architecture of the 11th and 12th centuries with a heavy appearance, blocky towers and rounded arches. Example: 34 Church Street South, Page 16	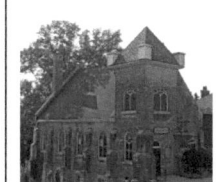
Saltbox: A saltbox is a building with a long, pitched roof that slopes down to the back, generally a wooden frame house. A saltbox has just one storey in the back and two stories in the front. The asymmetry of the unequal sides and the long, low rear roof line are the most distinctive features of a saltbox, which takes its name from its resemblance to a wooden lidded box in which salt was once kept. The earliest saltbox houses were created when a lean-to addition was added onto the rear of the original house extending the roof line sometimes to less than six feet from ground level. Example: 220 George Street, Page 39	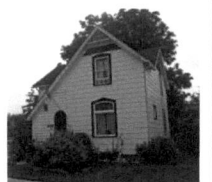
Second Empire, 1860-1880 – The mansard roof is the most noteworthy feature of this style and is evidence of the French origins. Projecting central towers and one or two-storey bays can also be present. Example: 236 Jones Street East, Page 44	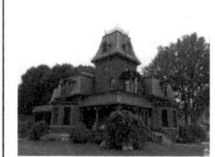
Tudor Revival – exposed timbers with stucco infill, multi-paned windows. Example: 218 Jones Street East, Page 43	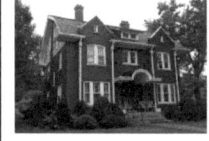